United States
Department of
Agriculture

Forest Service

Pacific Northwest
Research Station

General Technical
Report
PNW-GTR-709

June 2007

Potential Vegetation Hierarchy for the Blue Mountains Section of Northeastern Oregon, Southeastern Washington, and West-Central Idaho

David C. Powell, Charles G. Johnson, Jr., Elizabeth A. Crowe, Aaron Wells, and David K. Swanson

Authors

David C. Powell is a silviculturist, U.S. Department of Agriculture, Forest Service, Umatilla National Forest, 2517 SW Hailey Avenue, Pendleton, OR 97801; **Charles G. Johnson, Jr.** (deceased) was an area ecologist, U.S. Department of Agriculture, Forest Service, Wallowa-Whitman National Forest, P.O. Box 907, Baker City, OR 97814; **Elizabeth A. Crowe** is a vegetation ecologist, U.S. Department of the Interior, National Park Service, Greater Yellowstone Inventory and Monitoring Program, Box 173492, 229 AJM Johnson, Montana State University, Bozeman, MT 59717; **Aaron Wells** is a postdoctoral associate, Department of Ecology, 310 Lewis Hall, Montana State University, Bozeman, MT 59715; **David K. Swanson** is an area ecologist, U.S. Department of Agriculture, Forest Service, Wallowa-Whitman National Forest, P.O. Box 907, Baker City, OR 97814.

Cover Photo Credits

All photos by David C. Powell, show examples of the cool moist (top), warm dry (middle), and cold dry (bottom) upland forest plant associatioin groups.

Abstract

Powell, David C.; Johnson, Charles G., Jr.; Crowe, Elizabeth A.; Wells, Aaron; Swanson, David K. 2007. Potential vegetation hierarchy for the Blue Mountains section of northeastern Oregon, southeastern Washington, and west-central Idaho. Gen. Tech. Rep. PNW-GTR-709. Portland, OR: U.S. Department of Agriculture, Forest Service, Pacific Northwest Research Station. 87 p.

The work described in this report was initiated during the Interior Columbia Basin Ecosystem Management Project (ICBEMP). The ICBEMP produced a broad-scale scientific assessment of ecological, biophysical, social, and economic conditions for the interior Columbia River basin and portions of the Klamath and Great Basins. The broad-scale assessment made extensive use of potential vegetation (PV) information. This report (1) discusses certain concepts and terms as related to PV, (2) describes how a PV framework developed for the broad-scale ICBEMP assessment area was stepped down to the level of a single section in the national hierarchy of terrestrial ecological units, (3) describes how fine-scale potential vegetation types (PVTs) identified for the Blue Mountains section were aggregated into the midscale portion of the PV hierarchy, and (4) describes the PVT composition for each of the midscale hierarchical units (physiognomic class, potential vegetation group, plant association group).

Keywords: Potential vegetation, Blue Mountains, potential vegetation hierarchy, plant ecology, potential vegetation type, plant association group, physiognomic class, potential vegetation group.

Contents

Introduction

A distant summer view of the Blue Mountains shows a dark band of coniferous forest occurring above a lighter-colored grassland zone. Each of the two contrasting areas seems to be homogeneous, and the border between them appears sharp (Powell 2000).

A closer view reveals great diversity within each zone and borders that are poorly defined: herbaceous communities and stands of deciduous trees are scattered throughout the coniferous forest, and the species of dominant conifer changes from one site to another (Powell 2000).

At the foot of the Blue Mountains, fingers of forest and stands of tall deciduous shrubs invade the grassland zone for varying distances before becoming progressively less common and eventually disappearing altogether (Powell 2000).

This vegetation pattern demonstrates that the Blue Mountains are actually broken up into a myriad of small units, many of which repeat in an intricate, changing pattern. Making sense of this landscape mosaic is possible by using a concept called potential vegetation (PV) (Powell 2000).

Potential vegetation is defined as the community of plants that would become established if all successional sequences were completed, without interference by humans, under existing environmental conditions including edaphic, topographic, and climatic factors (Hall et al. 1995).[1] Potential vegetation, the theoretical endpoint of plant succession in the absence of disturbance, is used to characterize biophysical settings and their associated potential natural communities (Daubenmire 1968, Zerbe 1998).

This report describes a potential vegetation hierarchical analysis process initiated during the Interior Columbia Basin Ecosystem Management Project (ICBEMP). The ICBEMP began in January 1994 when the Chief of the USDA Forest Service (FS) and the Director of the USDI Bureau of Land Management (BLM) signed a charter; it directed that an ecosystem-based strategy be developed for management of FS and BLM lands within the project area.

The ICBEMP project area includes the U.S. portion of the interior Columbia River basin east of the crest of the Cascade Mountains in Oregon, Washington, Idaho, and western Montana, along with adjacent parts of Wyoming, Nevada, California, and Utah (some of the adjoining area includes portions of the Klamath and Great Basins). It contains over 145 million acres (58.7 million hectares), about

The Blue Mountains are actually broken up into a myriad of small units, many of which repeat in an intricate, changing pattern.

---

[1] Scientific and technical terms are defined in the glossary.

76 million acres (30.8 million hectares) of which are federal lands administered by the FS and BLM (Quigley and Arbelbide 1997, Quigley et al. 1996). At the time it was conducted, it was the largest assessment of its kind in the world (Quigley and Cole 1997).

The ICBEMP produced a framework for ecosystem management (Haynes et al. 1996) and a broad-scale assessment of ecological, biophysical, social, and economic conditions in the project area (Quigley and Arbelbide 1997, Quigley et al. 1996). The broad-scale assessment made extensive use of PV information (Jensen et al. 1997).

This report has four objectives:

- Discuss certain concepts and terms relating to PV–a glossary of terms is provided on page 36.
- Describe how the PV hierarchical framework developed for the ICBEMP broad-scale assessment was stepped down to the level of a single section (the Blue Mountains) in the national hierarchy of terrestrial ecological units.
- Describe how fine-scale potential vegetation types (PVTs) identified for the Blue Mountains section were aggregated into midscale PV hierarchical units.
- Describe the PVT composition for each of the midscale hierarchical units (physiognomic class, potential vegetation group, plant association group) in the Blue Mountains PV hierarchy.

Understanding different levels of resolution (e.g., scales) is central to an understanding of ecological capabilities and potentials.

Ecological Unit Hierarchy

Land and water areas have been classified into broad-scale hierarchies of aquatic and terrestrial ecological units (Bailey 1998, Maxwell et al. 1995). "The primary purpose for delineating ecological units is to identify land and water areas at different levels of resolution that have similar capabilities and potentials for management" (Cleland et al. 1997).

Understanding different levels of resolution (e.g., scales) is central to an understanding of ecological capabilities and potentials because ecosystem components (composition, structure, and function) are scale dependent (Levin 1992).

Eight levels are included in a national hierarchy of terrestrial ecological units, as adopted by the USDA Forest Service: domain, division, province, section, subsection, landtype association (LTA), landtype, and landtype phase (Cleland et al.

1997, McNab and Avers 1994). This report describes how a hierarchical PV process was implemented for a single section in the interior Pacific Northwest (section M332G, the Blue Mountains).

The broad-scale scientific assessment of the interior Columbia River basin and portions of the Klamath and Great Basins (Quigley and Arbelbide 1997, Quigley et al. 1996) included all or part of 7 provinces and 23 sections; only portions of some provinces or sections were included in the ICBEMP assessment area because its boundaries were established by using aquatic rather than terrestrial ecological units (Maxwell et al. 1995, Seaber et al. 1987).

Province M332, "middle Rocky Mountain steppe–coniferous forest–alpine meadow," is located in the Northwestern United States and includes parts of Oregon, Washington, Idaho, and Montana (Bailey 1998).

In the terrestrial ecological unit hierarchy, province M332 occurs in the "dry" domain and within a mountainous variant of the "temperate steppe" division (specifically, the "temperate steppe regime mountains") (McNab and Avers 1994).

Section M332G, the Blue Mountains, is the westernmost of seven sections in province M332 (Bailey 1998, McNab and Avers 1994).

At a regional scale, the Blue Mountains section consists of a series of mountain ranges occurring in a southwest to northeast orientation, extending from the Ochoco Mountains in central Oregon, the southwestern portion of the section, to the Seven Devils Mountains in west-central Idaho, the northeastern portion of the section (fig. 1).

This west to east orientation allows the Blue Mountains to function ecologically and floristically as a transverse bridge between the Cascade Mountains province to the west, and the main portion of the middle Rocky Mountains province to the east (Bryce and Omernik 1997, Rydberg 1916).

Naming Conventions

Potential vegetation types are traditionally referenced by using scientific plant names (e.g., *Pseudotsuga menziesii/Spiraea betulifolia*), common plant names (e.g., Douglas-fir/birchleaf spiraea), alphanumeric acronyms (e.g., PSME/SPBE2), and database codes (e.g., CDS634). (See "Species List" for common and scientific names and appendix tables 8 and 9 for potential vegetation types and codes.) When referring to a potential vegetation type in this report, the following naming conventions are used:

Figure 1—The Blue Mountains section. In the context of the national hierarchical framework of terrestrial ecological units (Cleland et al. 1997), the Blue Mountains are classified as section M332G; the Blue Mountains are the westernmost section in province M332: middle Rocky Mountain steppe–coniferous forest–alpine meadow (Bailey 1998, McNab and Avers 1994).

- Species in the same life form are separated with a dash (e.g., subalpine fir-whitebark pine), whereas species in different life forms are separated with a slash (e.g., grand fir/queencup beadlily).

- Alphanumeric acronyms are derived from scientific plant names: the first two letters of the genus name are combined with the first two letters of the species name and capitalized (e.g., ABGR for *Abies grandis*). If more than one species has the same code, then a number is added to differentiate between them (e.g., PIMO3 for *Pinus monticola*). The acronyms associated with the initial Blue Mountains potential vegetation classifications (Crowe and Clausnitzer 1997, Johnson and Clausnitzer 1992, Johnson and Simon 1987) were generally derived from Garrison et al. (1976).

- Nomenclature for scientific plant names was revised when the U.S. Department of Agriculture adopted a new national taxonomy called the PLANTS database (USDA NRCS 2004). In this report, the PLANTS codes are used for any plant species included in a Blue Mountains potential vegetation classification (Crowe and Clausnitzer 1997, Johnson 2004, Johnson and Clausnitzer 1992, Johnson and Simon 1987, Johnson and Swanson 2005, Wells 2006).

- For compatibility with Blue Mountains classifications published before the PLANTS database, the plant species codes used with the original reports, along with any PLANTS synonyms and synonym codes for these species, are provided in the species list ("R6 code"). Synonyms refer to instances where the PLANTS database has changed the original plant name to a new one. For example, *Stipa occidentalis* was the scientific name for western needlegrass in the original reports (Crowe and Clausnitzer 1997, Johnson and Clausnitzer 1992, Johnson and Simon 1987), but *Achnatherum occidentale occidentale* is the PLANTS scientific name for this species now (USDA NRCS 2004).

- All common names are shown in lower case letters except for proper names (e.g., Sandberg's bluegrass; Rocky Mountain maple).

- Ecoclass codes, used for recording PVTs on field forms and in databases, are described in Hall (1998, as supplemented); ecoclass codes for PVTs described in Blue Mountains potential vegetation classifications are provided in appendix tables 8 and 9.

Potential Vegetation Concepts

The genetic characteristics of a plant species allow it to be adapted to a specific range of environmental conditions, which is called its ecological amplitude (Daubenmire 1968). Ecological amplitude controls how a plant species interacts with physical site factors such as altitude (elevation), aspect, geology, and soil type. Together these factors create the underlying foundation, a geomorphic template, upon which the biological landscape is constructed.

Physical and other abiotic factors govern belowground ecosystem processes (such as nutrient cycling) and create aboveground gradients in productivity, structure, and composition. Does this mean that the abundance or distribution of a potential natural community is controlled exclusively by elevation, rock type, or any other individual factor? In general, the answer to this question is "no."

Potential vegetation can be thought of as the algebraic sum of all environmental factors influencing the flora of an area (Daubenmire 1976). The physical factors of a plant's environment interact to form a temperature and moisture regime influenced primarily by gradients of elevation, slope steepness and configuration, aspect, and geologic parent materials and their resulting soils (Kruckeberg 2002, Meurisse et al. 1991, Swanson et al. 1988, Westveld 1951). These site factors interact by complementing or counteracting each other, so any individual factor has limited influence by itself.

Potential vegetation can be thought of as the algebraic sum of all environmental factors influencing the flora of an area.

The concept of complementary factors is illustrated by the situation where a plant community occurs on different aspects as elevation changes. At a low elevation within its distribution, a plant community may grow on a steep, north-facing slope because this combination of environmental factors results in cooler and moister conditions than are typical for the elevation. At intermediate portions of its elevational range, a plant community tends to be at an optimum and it then occurs on zonal soils and moderate aspects (east- or west-facing exposures). At high elevations, it may be found on a steep, south-facing slope because this combination of environmental factors results in warmer and dryer conditions than typically prevail for the altitude (Blumer 1911, Daubenmire 1952).

This example demonstrates that plant species seldom have the same ecological indicator status wherever they occur. Land managers should be able to interpret the indicator status of the plant species and communities with which they work (Westveld 1951). This skill is particularly important when working with mixed-species communities (Powell 2000).

The presence of ponderosa pine in stands trending toward domination by grand fir, for example, may indicate only that one or more mature ponderosa pines happened to be within seed dissemination distance when the last wildfire or other disturbance event occurred. How would a land manager come to that conclusion?

Shade-intolerant tree species such as ponderosa pine can colonize sites that are moister than they can hold onto when facing competition from shade-tolerant species such as grand fir; ponderosa pine and grand fir occurring together on the grand fir/twinflower plant association is an example of this situation for the Blue Mountains section (Johnson and Clausnitzer 1992).

This species occurrence pattern suggests that varying proportions of ponderosa pine and grand fir may not indicate changes in temperature or moisture relationships (ponderosa pine indicating warm and dry microsites; grand fir indicating cool and moist microsites), but may instead represent an expected progression in a post-disturbance sere where early-seral ponderosa pine is gradually being replaced by late-seral grand fir (Daubenmire 1966).

This example illustrates that the proportion of ponderosa pine in a mixed-conifer stand may have limited indicator value with respect to a site's temperature and moisture status, but it might be useful as an indicator of how much time has passed since the last wildfire or other disturbance event with sufficient intensity to initiate a cohort of early-seral tree species (Daubenmire 1966).

Potential vegetation implies that over long periods and in the absence of disturbance, similar types of plant communities (PVTs) will develop on similar sites. Knowing which PVT will develop is useful because it indicates ecological site potential (Cook 1996, Westveld 1951) and helps predict ecosystem response to disturbance processes such as wildfire (Brown et al. 2004, Crane and Fischer 1986, Franklin and Agee 2003, Hann et al. 2005) and invasive species (Despain et al. 2001, Weaver et al. 2001).

Potential vegetation offers insights about inherent productivity and other vegetation-site relationships (Meurisse et al. 1991), is valuable for projecting plant succession pathways (Beukema et al. 2003, Clausnitzer 1993, Kurz et al. 2000), and helps put the existing vegetation patterns of an area into an ecological context (Daubenmire 1966, 1976).

Potential vegetation offers insights about inherent productivity and other vegetation-site relationships.

Potential Versus Existing Vegetation

The occurrence of ponderosa pine and grand fir in mixed stands demonstrates an important difference between potential vegetation and existing vegetation. Potential vegetation describes the floristic composition produced in a disturbance-free environment and under existing climatic conditions, and it accounts for internal or autogenic changes occurring during plant succession (soil changes, nutrient cycling, etc.).

Classifying vegetation by assuming that disturbance is absent, might seem irrelevant in the interior Columbia River basin where disturbance processes are ubiquitous (Hann et al. 1997, Losensky 1994), but this classification concept identifies the most competitive plant species **in the context of existing climate,** and they can then function as useful indicators of a site's ecological potential (Pfister and Arno 1980).

Because classification describes the plant composition associated with recent historical and existing climate, the composition and distribution of PVTs is expected to change as climate changes. Climate change modeling for the broad-scale scientific assessment of the interior Columbia River basin and portions of the Klamath and Great Basins predicted that with a doubling of atmospheric carbon dioxide levels, the *Thuja plicata/Clintonia uniflora* (western redcedar/queencup beadlily) plant association would occur in the Blue Mountains section even though it does not occur there now (Jensen et al. 1997).

In the pine-fir, mixed-species plant community example described above, ponderosa pine will not ultimately prevail because grand fir is more competitive in the absence of disturbance. When considering the PV concept established by Daubenmire (1968), Pfister and Arno (1980), and many others, this means that grand fir is a more useful indicator species than ponderosa pine because the classification objective is to identify the dominant composition associated with climate and other abiotic conditions, not with stochastic factors such as disturbance (McCune and Allen 1985a, 1985b). In other words, this concept recognizes that plant associations are distinct entities varying in response to biophysical site factors, not just random groupings of plants brought together by chance (Westveld 1951).

In the interior Pacific Northwest, fire and other disturbance processes usually intervene to prevent development of climax plant communities (Agee 1993, 1998; Habeck and Mutch 1973), but knowledge about life history traits and vital attributes allows us to predict a site's potential floristic composition (Huston and Smith 1987, Noble and Slatyer 1980, Roberts 1996). This is why the concept is referred to as potential vegetation—certain site characteristics (the physical and abiotic environment), in combination with the presence or absence of diagnostic indicator plants, provide clues about the potential composition of an area's vegetation (the climax plant community) (Powell 2000).

Potential vegetation is an indicator of the environmental gradients controlling vegetation dynamics—it reflects how shade-tolerant and shade-intolerant tree species develop and interact in mixed forests (Smith and Huston 1989); the rate at which ecosystems produce and accumulate biomass (Daubenmire 1976); and the potential impact of fire, insects, pathogens, and other disturbance processes on forest composition and structure (McDonald 1991, Powell 2005, Schmitt and Powell 2005, Steele et al. 1996).

The management implications of plant succession, forest growth, and other ecosystem processes are predictable (within limits) because they can be related to PV, and sites with similar PV tend to respond to disturbance processes in a similar way (Cook 1996, Daubenmire 1961). For this reason, the "fire regime condition class" protocol (Hann et al. 2005) and several other assessment or mapping processes (Comer et al. 2003, Küchler 1964) have adopted a PV concept explicitly incorporating natural or historical disturbance.

Existing vegetation differs from PV because it represents conditions as they exist today—what a land manager finds on the ground and deals with on a daily basis (Brohman and Bryant 2005). Historically, natural resource management was based on classifications of existing vegetation (e.g., Eyre 1980, Shiflet 1994). Although maps displaying existing vegetation provide valuable information about current composition and structure, they supply little insight about site productivity and other management implications (Daubenmire 1973, Deitschmann 1973, Westveld 1951).

This means that the two classification approaches—PV and existing vegetation—tend to be used in different ways and for different purposes: existing vegetation is well suited for meeting operational needs because it represents "what is" (current conditions), whereas PV is ideally suited for planning and assessment processes because it represents "what could be" (ecological site potential) (Powell 2000, Westveld 1951).

Potential Vegetation Classification

Ecosystems are complexes of living organisms interacting with each other and their environment. There are many kinds of ecosystems but not an infinite number, and ecologists have learned that similar ecosystems occur repeatedly across the landscape (Klinka and Carter 1980). Vegetation is a readily observed component of an ecosystem. It can be used to characterize floristic communities and to help map aquatic and terrestrial ecological units (Bailey 1996).

The process of delineating and characterizing floristic communities is called vegetation classification. Potential vegetation is classified by using a taxonomic approach of sampling stands with climax or late-successional plant composition. These classifications are based on the concept that a community of plants proceeds through successional pathways to a potential climax association that is typical or characteristic of a particular biophysical environment (Pfister and Arno 1980).

Grouping similar PVTs results in a taxonomic hierarchy. For the Blue Mountains section, PV has been organized as one hierarchy consisting of two integrated portions—the fine-scale hierarchical units are useful for operational or project-level planning (Emmingham et al. 2005, Hall 1989), and the midscale hierarchical units are suitable for ecosystem analysis at the watershed scale (REO 1995) and for other strategic purposes (Johnson et al. 1999) (fig. 2).

The midscale taxonomic units have been particularly useful for ecological mapping. Plant association groups resulting from a temperature-moisture classification framework (Jensen et al. 1997, Powell 1998), along with information about geomorphology, geologic rock types, soil complexes, and other abiotic components, were used as the PV component or element when mapping landtype associations (LTAs) for national forests of the Blue Mountains section during 2003 and 2004 (Winthers et al. 2005).

Landtype association is one of the categorical classification units within the national hierarchy of terrestrial ecological units (Cleland et al. 1997, McNab and Avers 1994). The mapping unit for LTAs is based primarily on landforms, surficial geology, and midscale taxonomic units for soils and PV (Winthers et al. 2005).

Existing vegetation is well suited for meeting operational needs because it represents "what is," whereas potential vegetation is ideally suited for planning and assessment processes because it represents "what could be."

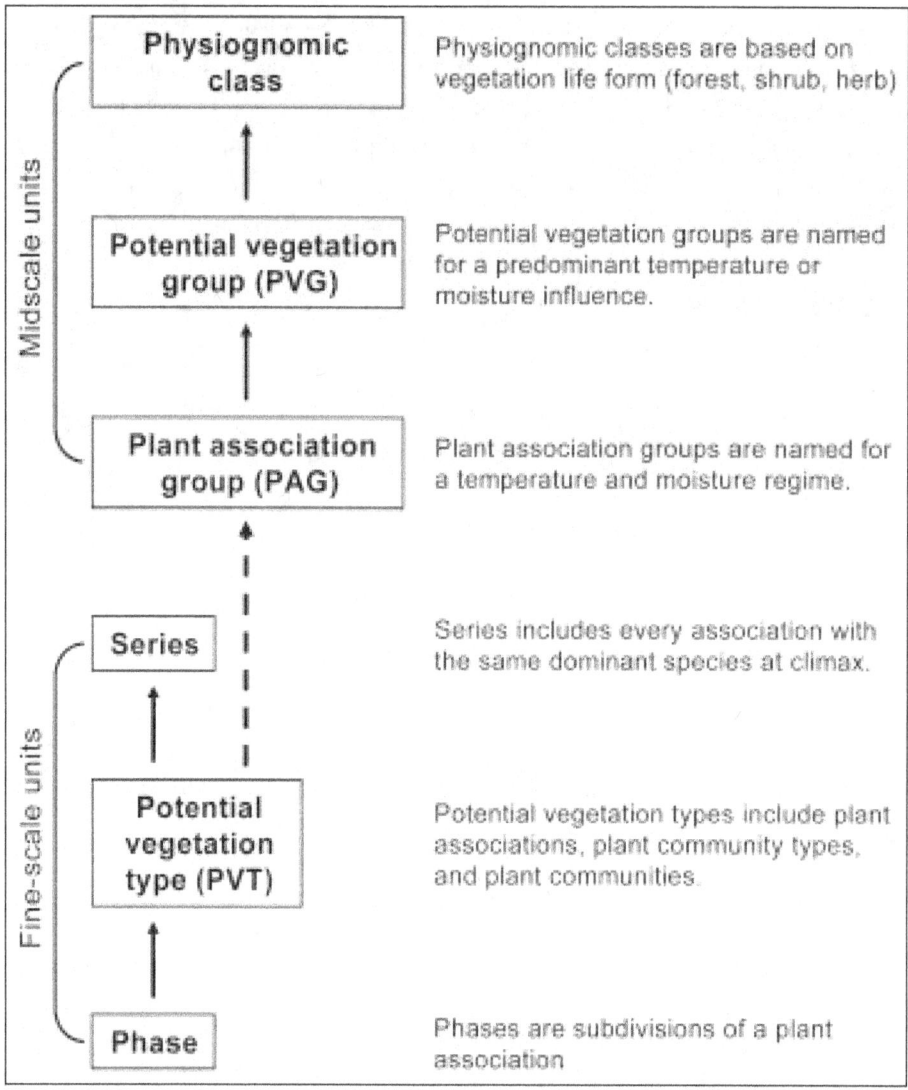

Figure 2—Hierarchy of potential vegetation (PV) for the Blue Mountains section (figure adapted from Powell 2000). The PV taxonomic units have been organized as two integrated portions of a PV hierarchy. The fine-scale hierarchical units are described in PV classification reports and their associated keys (Crowe and Clausnitzer 1997, Johnson 2004, Johnson and Clausnitzer 1992, Johnson and Simon 1987, Johnson and Swanson 2005, and Wells 2006). Potential vegetation types (PVTs) provide a link between the fine-scale and midscale portions of the PV hierarchy because PVTs are aggregated to form plant association groups.

During mapping of LTAs for the Blue Mountains section, it was found that fine-scale PV units (particularly PVTs as defined in this report) were at too fine a scale to be useful, but that midscale units (particularly potential vegetation groups) provided a reasonable level of discrimination when delineating LTA mapping units in the field.

Predictive mapping of PV has many useful applications for ecosystem planning and management (Deitschmann 1973, Kelly et al. 2005). A recent classification-tree modeling project used geographic information system (GIS) layers for topography, slope position, geology and soils, solar radiation, and precipitation and topographic moisture in a map-overlay computer processing environment (Bailey 1996) to predict plant associations, plant association groups, and vegetation series for a large study area in northeastern Oregon. The midscale plant association groups (and the other predicted units) were then mappable in GIS. Note that for this modeling project, all predicted units of PV pertained exclusively to upland types because riparian types function at a different (finer) scale, and it is seldom possible to discriminate between them in a modeling or GIS context (Kelly et al. 2005).

Each unique combination of abiotic factors results in a slightly different temperature and moisture regime.

Potential Vegetation Hierarchy
Fine-Scale Hierarchical Units

Literally thousands of plant species call the Blue Mountains home (Botanical Resources Group 2004, Hanson 2000). The vegetation of a region tends to reflect the types of habitat that are available to it, and the Blue Mountains provide a diversity of habitat owing to variation in landforms, topography, climate, soils, slope exposure, geologic parent materials, and other abiotic factors. The almost limitless combination of these abiotic factors offers a vast array of habitats where plants can become established and grow (Clarke and Bryce 1997).

Each unique combination of abiotic factors results in a slightly different temperature and moisture regime. Ecological amplitude controls how plants interact with abiotic factors. As plant occurrence and distribution are influenced primarily by temperature and moisture, when abiotic factors vary enough to modify the temperature and moisture regime, they cause a change in plant composition (Sampson 1939).

In the Blue Mountains section, temperature and moisture regimes vary somewhat predictably with changes in elevation, aspect, and slope exposure (Kelly et al. 2005). This variation across biophysical settings is consistent with our current understanding of the environmental tolerances (life history traits and vital attributes) for the dominant plant species (McCook 1994, Powell 2000).

One objective of PV classification is to delineate relatively homogeneous units of biophysical environment. Each biophysical environment is characterized by its potential floristic composition. The biophysical environments of an area are described in PV classifications (e.g., Crowe and Clausnitzer 1997, Johnson 2004, Johnson and Clausnitzer 1992, Johnson and Simon 1987, Johnson and Swanson 2005, and Wells 2006, for the Blue Mountains section).

The PV classifications not only define the fine-scale PV hierarchical units of an area (Pfister and Arno 1980), but they also provide dichotomous keys to aid in their identification.

Series—

The highest level of the fine-scale portion of the PV hierarchy is based on the dominant climax plant species and is called the series (fig. 2). The subalpine fir series, for example, includes every plant association where subalpine fir is presumed to be the dominant tree species at climax. The series unit of the PV hierarchy is assumed to reflect macroclimatic conditions at the site scale.

Potential vegetation types—

The middle level of the fine-scale portion of the PV hierarchy (fig. 2) is defined by using one or more species from the dominant (overstory) vegetation layer and one or more indicator plants from the subordinate (undergrowth) layer. This hierarchical unit is the PVT. The PVTs include three of the taxonomic units described in PV classifications for the Blue Mountains section: plant associations,[2] plant community types, and plant communities.

Plant associations—

Plant associations are named for their dominant overstory and undergrowth plants, such as the *Abies grandis/Clintonia uniflora* plant association (abbreviated ABGR/CLUN2).

---

[2] For much of the Western United States, the lowest level of the fine-scale portion of the potential vegetation hierarchy is called a "habitat type" instead of a plant association. There is actually little distinction between the two terms because a habitat type refers to the physical environment (land area) having the capability to support a particular plant association; habitat types are named for the climax plant communities (plant associations) they can support. In other words, habitat types are land-mapping units; plant associations can be thought of as their attributes, legend items, or map labels (Alexander 1985).

From an ecological perspective, it is assumed that the dominant (overstory) species of a plant association reflects macroclimate at a site scale, whereas the subordinate indicator plants represent an area's microclimate and soils. For the *Abies grandis/Clintonia uniflora* plant association, *Abies grandis* is assumed to reflect the macroclimatic regime, whereas *Clintonia uniflora* is responding to microclimatic conditions.

The land area capable of supporting a plant association (the habitat type) is considered to be fairly homogeneous in terms of its growing environment, and it integrates site-scale variability in elevation, soil, geology, and other abiotic factors in such a way that the same climax overstory and understory vegetation will eventually be produced (Davis et al. 2001).

Plant community types—
Some late-seral vegetation types persist on the landscape and have been referred to as plant community types in PV classifications (Johnson and Clausnitzer 1992). This taxonomic unit includes vegetation that might be climax but about which there is uncertainty. Plant community types occur repeatedly across the landscape, but they are considered to be successional to one or more plant associations.

Plant community types are named in much the same way as plant associations: they use a binomial name consisting of one or more of the dominant (overstory) species and one or more of the subordinate (undergrowth) plants.

For plant community types, the undergrowth indicator plants are typically assumed to represent the climax composition, whereas the overstory dominants are often early- or midseral species that have not yet been supplanted by late-seral or potential natural community species (Hall et al. 1995).

Early- or midseral tree species can dominate plant community types when their longevity exceeds that of the late-seral, shade-tolerant species, or because they possess a set of life history traits (such as thick bark and low bark resin) (Flint 1925, Starker 1934) rendering them particularly well suited to a stand-maintaining disturbance regime such as frequent surface fire (McCook 1994).

Plant communities—
Some PV classifications also include a taxonomic unit called plant communities. Vegetation types designated as a plant community have no particular successional (seral) status. Generally, plant communities are vegetation types with a limited distribution in the geographical area covered by the classification, or they were described by using such a small number of sample plots that it is not possible to infer their true successional status (Johnson and Clausnitzer 1992).

Phases—

The lowest level of the fine-scale portion of the PV hierarchy is called a phase, which represents a subdivision of a plant association (fig. 2). Phases reflect minor environmental differences within a plant association and are named for an indicator species, such as the pinegrass phase of the Douglas-fir/birchleaf spiraea plant association (PSME/SPBE2, CARU phase) (Steele et al. 1981).

Although commonly used elsewhere in the Rocky Mountains (Alexander 1985, Pfister and Arno 1980), phases were not included in PV classifications for the Blue Mountains section (Crowe and Clausnitzer 1997, Johnson 2004, Johnson and Clausnitzer 1992, Johnson and Simon 1987, Johnson and Swanson 2005, Wells 2006).

Midscale Hierarchical Units

Once an area has been classified and mapped into PVTs (plant associations, plant community types, plant communities), this fine-scale information can then be aggregated to make it useful for midscale analysis and assessment purposes (Bergeron and Bouchard 1984). Although aggregation has potential pitfalls (oversimplification often does more harm than good), it can provide clarity and foster strategic thinking: "we must learn how to aggregate and simplify, retaining essential information, without getting bogged down in unnecessary detail" (Levin 1992).

Potential vegetation information is useful for a variety of midscale purposes such as these:

- Land and resource management planning (Emmingham et al. 2005, Hall 1989)
- Ecosystem analysis at the watershed scale (REO 1995)
- Bioregional assessments such as the Interior Columbia Basin Ecosystem Management Project (Johnson et al. 1999)
- Assessing wildland fire susceptibility (Graham et al. 2004, Huff et al. 1995, Peterson et al. 2005, Powell 2005, Schmidt et al. 2002)
- Characterizing suggested tree stocking levels (Cochran et al. 1994, Powell 1999).

To support the strategic needs described above, fine-scale PV information for the Blue Mountains section was aggregated into midscale PV hierarchical units (fig. 2).

> Although aggregation has potential pitfalls, it can provide clarity and foster strategic thinking.

Midscale PV information provides an ideal framework for characterizing the dynamic nature of plant succession and for explicitly recognizing the need to manage vegetation at a broad geographical scale. A midscale approach also results in more congruence between inherent patterns of ecological site potential and native disturbance regimes (Everett and Lehmkuhl 1999).

The midscale portion of the PV hierarchy has three levels: physiognomic classes, potential vegetation groups (PVGs), and plant association groups (PAGs). As PVTs (e.g., plant associations, plant community types, plant communities) are aggregated to form PAGs, PVTs provide a link between the fine- and midscale portions of the PV hierarchy (fig. 2).

Temperature-Moisture Approach

At a broad scale, PV varies along an environmental gradient reflecting the interaction of landform, topography, climate, geology, and other macro-scale factors (Daubenmire 1968, 1976). At a fine scale, however, the environmental gradient is controlled by site-level factors such as elevation, slope steepness and configuration (convex, flat, concave), and slope direction (aspect) (Jensen et al. 1997).

In its simplest form, a midscale environmental gradient can be defined by using two characteristics integrating environmental factors: temperature and moisture. This classification framework relies on the premise that physiognomically dominant species, such as those used to define a fine-scale hierarchical unit called the series (see fig. 2), indicate a temperature gradient and that subordinate species, such as shrubs and herbs found on the forest floor in a conifer-dominated community, indicate a moisture gradient.

By using temperature and moisture as a classification framework, PVTs can be arrayed in two-dimensional space, showing not only their relationship to relative gradients of temperature and moisture but also to other PVTs found in the same geographical area.

Physiognomic Classes

Although the temperature-moisture matrix approach is intuitively attractive, it is difficult to adequately represent the vegetation diversity of the Blue Mountains and other large landmasses in a single temperature-moisture matrix. After reaching that conclusion, we refined the temperature-moisture approach for the Blue Mountains section in a three-step process:

1. The vegetation was initially divided into three broad physiognomic classes: forest, shrub, and herb (herb includes both grasses and forbs).[3] This division was made to acknowledge that temperature and moisture gradients differ for each class—what is considered warm in a forest setting differs from warm for herb environments.

2. The initial division into three physiognomic classes resulted in too much variation to adequately meet midscale needs, particularly with respect to moisture. Therefore, the initial classes were divided again to better represent their moisture variability. This step established upland and riparian variants for each of the original classes: upland and riparian forest, upland and riparian shrub, and upland and riparian herb.

3. A final division was made to separate a woodland physiognomic class (consisting of western juniper plant associations) from the remainder of the upland forest physiognomic class. This division was made to explicitly recognize that juniper woodlands represent important differences in vegetation structure and function when compared with other PVTs having forest physiognomy.

This process resulted in establishment of seven physiognomic classes, each of which has its own temperature-moisture matrix:

- Upland forest, upland woodland, upland shrub, and upland herb;
- Riparian forest, riparian shrub, and riparian herb.

Temperature-Moisture Matrix (Plant Association Groups)

By delineating multiple categories of temperature, and by doing the same for moisture, a temperature-moisture matrix was developed for use with the physiognomic classes. This matrix framework was initially developed for a broad-scale scientific assessment of the interior Columbia River basin and portions of the Klamath and Great Basins; the matrices were used when characterizing biophysical environments of the basin (Jensen et al. 1997, Reid et al. 1995).

The temperature-moisture matrix provides a convenient ecological framework for aggregating fine-scale PVTs into what is termed plant association groups.[4] This

> **The temperature-moisture matrix provides a convenient ecological framework for aggregating fine-scale PVTs into what is termed plant association groups.**

---

[3] This stratification into three physiognomic classes was identical to the potential vegetation classification framework developed for the interior Columbia River basin scientific assessment (Jensen et al. 1997, Reid et al. 1995).

[4] Sometimes, plant association groups (PAGs) are assumed to be equivalent to biophysical environments. This assumption is seldom true because the delineation criteria for biophysical environments typically incorporate physical or abiotic factors such as geology or geomorphology explicitly (Jensen et al. 1997), whereas PAGs are delineated by using potential vegetation types only.

means that each cell in a temperature-moisture matrix represents a unique plant association group. Plant association groups are the lowest level of the midscale portion of the PV hierarchy established for the Blue Mountains section (fig. 2).

For the upland physiognomic classes, a 4-row by 4-column (16-cell) matrix consisting of four categories of temperature (cold, cool, warm, hot) and 4 categories of moisture (wet, very moist, moist, dry) was adopted (table 1).[5]

Assignment of upland PVTs to physiognomic temperature-moisture matrices is presented for the four upland physiognomic classes (table 2).

For the riparian physiognomic classes, three categories of soil moisture were found to be more ecologically relevant than the four classes of ambient (site) moisture used for the upland types (Manning and Engelking 1997). Therefore, the riparian matrices used four categories of temperature (the same ones used for the upland matrices) and three categories of soil moisture.

The three categories of riparian soil moisture were identical to the three "riparian moisture phases" used when developing riparian PV settings for a broad-scale scientific assessment of the interior Columbia River basin and portions of the Klamath and Great Basins (Jensen et al. 1997, Manning and Engelking 1997).

For the riparian physiognomic classes, a 4-row by 3-column (12-cell) matrix consisting of four categories of temperature (cold, cool, warm, hot) and three categories of soil moisture (high, moderate, low) was adopted (table 3).

Table 1—A 16-cell matrix of temperature and moisture categories

	Moisture			
Temperature	**Wet**	**Very moist**	**Moist**	**Dry**
Cold	Cold wet	Cold very moist	Cold moist	Cold dry
Cool	Cool wet	Cool very moist	Cool moist	Cool dry
Warm	Warm wet	Warm very moist	Warm moist	Warm dry
Hot	Hot wet	Hot very moist	Hot moist	Hot dry

A 4 by 4 temperature-moisture matrix like the one shown here was used for the four physiognomic classes included in table 2: upland forest, upland woodland, upland shrub, and upland herb. The fine-scale potential vegetation types occurring in an upland physiognomic class were assigned to one, and only one, of the class's matrix cells. Individual matrix cells (warm dry, cool wet, etc.) are used as plant association groups in the midscale portion of the potential vegetation hierarchy (fig. 2).

---

[5] The temperature and moisture categories are roughly analogous to soil temperature and moisture regimes used for soil taxonomy and classification (Meurisse et al. 1991, USDA NRCS 2003), but they are not directly comparable category to category. Soil temperature and moisture regimes are defined by using criteria that incorporate timing of moisture and temperature with respect to plant growing seasons.

Table 2–Potential vegetation groups (PVG), plant association groups (PAG), and potential vegetation type (PVT) codes and common names for upland physiognomic classes

PVG	PAG	PVT code (PLANTS code)	PVT common name
Cold upland forest	Cold moist	ABLA/MEFE	subalpine fir/rusty menziesia
		ABLA/RHAL2	subalpine fir/white rhododendron
		ABLA-PIEN/LEGL	subalpine fir-Engelmann spruce/Labrador tea
		ABLA-PIEN/MEFE	subalpine fir-Engelmann spruce/rusty menziesia
		ABLA-PIEN/RHAL2	subalpine fir-Engelmann spruce/white rhododendron
		ABLA-PIEN/SETR	subalpine fir-Engelmann spruce/arrowleaf groundsel
	Cold dry	ABGR/ARCO9	grand fir/heartleaf arnica
		ABGR/VASC	grand fir/grouse huckleberry
		ABLA/CAGE2	subalpine fir/elk sedge
		ABLA/FEVI	subalpine fir/green fescue
		ABLA/JUDR	subalpine fir/Drummond's rush
		ABLA/JUPA (AVALANCHE)	subalpine fir/Parry's rush (avalanche)
		ABLA/JUTE	subalpine fir/slender rush
		ABLA/POPH	subalpine fir/alpine fleeceflower
		ABLA/POPU3	subalpine fir/Jacob's ladder
		ABLA/STOC2	subalpine fir/western needlegrass
		ABLA/VASC	subalpine fir/grouse huckleberry
		ABLA/VASC-PHEM	subalpine fir/grouse huckleberry-pink mountainheath
		ABLA/VASC/POPU3	subalpine fir/grouse huckleberry/Jacob's ladder
		ABLA-PIAL/ARAC2	subalpine fir-whitebark pine/prickly sandwort
		ABLA-PIAL/CAGE2	subalpine fir-whitebark pine/elk sedge
		ABLA-PIAL/FEVI	subalpine fir-whitebark pine/green fescue
		ABLA-PIAL/JUCO6	subalpine fir-whitebark pine/mountain juniper
		ABLA-PIAL/JUCO6-ARNE	subalpine fir-whitebark pine/mountain juniper-pinemat manzanita
		ABLA-PIAL/JUDR	subalpine fir-whitebark pine/Drummond's rush
		ABLA-PIAL/JUPA-STLE2	subalpine fir-whitebark pine/Parry's rush-Lemmon's needlegrass
		ABLA-PIAL/POPH	subalpine fir-whitebark pine/alpine fleeceflower
		ABLA-PIAL/POPU3	subalpine fir-whitebark pine/Jacob's ladder
		ABLA-PIAL/RIMO2/POPU3	subalpine fir-whitebark pine/mountain gooseberry/Jacob's ladder
		ABLA-PIAL/VASC/ARAC2	subalpine fir-whitebark pine/grouse huckleberry/prickly sandwort
		ABLA-PIAL/VASC/ARCO9	subalpine fir-whitebark pine/grouse huckleberry/heartleaf arnica
		ABLA-PIAL/VASC/CARO5	subalpine fir-whitebark pine/grouse huckleberry/Ross' sedge
		ABLA-PIAL/VASC/FEVI*	subalpine fir-whitebark pine/grouse huckleberry/green fescue
		ABLA-PIAL/VASC/LECOW2	subalpine fir-whitebark pine/grouse huckleberry/Wallowa Lewisia
		ABLA-PIAL/VASC/OREX	subalpine fir-whitebark pine/grouse huckleberry/little ricegrass
		ABLA-PIAL/VASC-PHEM*	subalpine fir-whitebark pine/grouse huckleberry-pink mountainheath
		ABLA-PIEN/LUHI4	subalpine fir-Engelmann spruce/smooth woodrush
		ABLA-PIEN/POPU3	subalpine fir-Engelmann spruce/Jacob's ladder
		ABLA-PIEN/VASC-PHEM	subalpine fir-Engelmann spruce/grouse huckleberry-pink mountainheath
		PIAL/ARAC2	whitebark pine/prickly sandwort
		PIAL/CAGE2	whitebark pine/elk sedge
		PIAL/FEVI	whitebark pine/green fescue
		PIAL/JUCO6-ARNE	whitebark pine/mountain juniper-pinemat manzanita
		PIAL/LUAR3	whitebark pine/silvery lupine
		PIAL/RIMO2/POPU3	whitebark pine/mountain gooseberry/Jacob's ladder
		PIAL/VASC/ARAC2	whitebark pine/grouse huckleberry/prickly sandwort
		PIAL/VASC/ARCO9	whitebark pine/grouse huckleberry/heartleaf arnica
		PIAL/VASC/LUHI4	whitebark pine/grouse huckleberry/smooth woodrush
		PICO(ABGR)/VASC/CARU	lodgepole pine(grand fir)/grouse huckleberry/pinegrass

Table 2–Potential vegetation groups (PVG), plant association groups (PAG), and potential vegetation type (PVT) codes and common names for upland physiognomic classes (continued)

PVG	PAG	PVT code (PLANTS code)	PVT common name
Cold upland forest	Cold dry	PICO(ABLA)/CAGE2	lodgepole pine(subalpine fir)/elk sedge
		PICO(ABLA)/STOC2	lodgepole pine(subalpine fir)/western needlegrass
		PICO(ABLA)/VASC	lodgepole pine(subalpine fir)/grouse huckleberry
		PICO(ABLA)/VASC/POPU3	lodgepole pine(subalpine fir)/grouse huckleberry/Jacob's ladder
		PIFL2/JUCO6	limber pine/mountain juniper
		PSME/RIMO2/POPU3	Douglas-fir/mountain gooseberry/Jacob's ladder
		TSME/VAME	mountain hemlock/big huckleberry
		TSME/VASC	mountain hemlock/grouse huckleberry
	Cool dry	ABGR/COOC	grand fir/goldthread
		ABLA/ARNE/ARAC2	subalpine fir/pinemat manzanita/prickly sandwort
		ABLA/CARU	subalpine fir/pinegrass
		ABLA/XETE	subalpine fir/beargrass
		ABLA-PIMO3/CHUM	subalpine fir-western white pine/prince's pine
		PICO/CARU	lodgepole pine/pinegrass
		PICO(ABGR)/ARNE	lodgepole pine(grand fir)/pinemat manzanita
		PICO(ABGR)/CARU	lodgepole pine(grand fir)/pinegrass
Moist upland forest	Cool wet	ABGR/TABR2/CLUN2*	grand fir/Pacific yew/queencup beadlily
		ABGR/TABR2/LIBO3	grand fir/Pacific yew/twinflower
		ABLA/STAM2	subalpine fir/claspleaf twistedstalk
	Cool very moist	ABGR/GYDR	grand fir/oakfern
		ABGR/POMU-ASCA2	grand fir/swordfern-ginger
		ABGR/TRCA	grand fir/false bugbane
		PICO(ABGR)/ALSI3	lodgepole pine(grand fir)/Sitka alder
		POTR5/CAGE2	quaking aspen/elk sedge
	Cool moist	ABGR/CLUN2	grand fir/queencup beadlily
		ABGR/LIBO3*	grand fir/twinflower
		ABGR/VAME*	grand fir/big huckleberry
		ABGR/VASC-LIBO3	grand fir/grouse huckleberry-twinflower
		ABGR-CHNO/VAME	grand fir-Alaska yellow cedar/big huckleberry
		ABLA/ARCO9*	subalpine fir/heartleaf arnica
		ABLA/CLUN2*	subalpine fir/queencup beadlily
		ABLA/LIBO3*	subalpine fir/twinflower
		ABLA/TRCA	subalpine fir/false bugbane
		ABLA/VAME*	subalpine fir/big huckleberry
		ABLA-PIEN/ARCO9	subalpine fir-Engelmann spruce/heartleaf arnica
		ABLA-PIEN/CLUN2	subalpine fir-Engelmann spruce/queencup beadlily
		ABLA-PIEN/LIBO3	subalpine fir-Engelmann spruce/twinflower
		ABLA-PIEN/TRCA	subalpine fir-Engelmann spruce/false bugbane
		PICO(ABGR)/LIBO3	lodgepole pine(grand fir)/twinflower
		PICO(ABGR)/VAME	lodgepole pine(grand fir)/big huckleberry
		PICO(ABGR)/VAME/CARU	lodgepole pine(grand fir)/big huckleberry/pinegrass
		PICO(ABGR)/VAME/PTAQ	lodgepole pine(grand fir)/big huckleberry/bracken fern
		PICO(ABGR)/VAME-LIBO3	lodgepole pine(grand fir)/big huckleberry-twinflower
		PICO(ABLA)/VAME*	lodgepole pine(subalpine fir)/big huckleberry
		PICO(ABLA)/VAME/CARU	lodgepole pine(subalpine fir)/big huckleberry/pinegrass

Table 2–Potential vegetation groups (PVG), plant association groups (PAG), and potential vegetation type (PVT) codes and common names for upland physiognomic classes (continued)

PVG	PAG	PVT code (PLANTS code)	PVT common name
Moist upland forest	Warm very moist	ABGR/ACGL*	grand fir/Rocky Mountain maple
	Warm moist	ABGR/ACGL-PHMA5	grand fir/Rocky Mountain maple-mallow ninebark
		ABGR/BRVU	grand fir/Columbia brome
		PSME/ACGL-PHMA5	Douglas-fir/Rocky Mountain maple-mallow ninebark
		PSME/ACGL-SYOR2	Douglas-fir/Rocky Mountain maple-mountain snowberry
		PSME/HODI	Douglas-fir/oceanspray
Dry upland forest	Warm dry	ABGR/CAGE2	grand fir/elk sedge
		ABGR/CARU*	grand fir/pinegrass
		ABGR/SPBE2*	grand fir/birchleaf spiraea
		JUSC2/CELE3	Rocky Mountain juniper/mountain mahogany
		PIPO/CAGE2	ponderosa pine/elk sedge
		PIPO/CARU	ponderosa pine/pinegrass
		PIPO/CELE3/CAGE2	ponderosa pine/mountain mahogany/elk sedge
		PIPO/PUTR2/CAGE2	ponderosa pine/bitterbrush/elk sedge
		PIPO/PUTR2/CARO5	ponderosa pine/bitterbrush/Ross' sedge
		PIPO/SPBE2	ponderosa pine/birchleaf spiraea
		PIPO/SYAL*	ponderosa pine/common snowberry
		PIPO/SYOR2	ponderosa pine/mountain snowberry
		PSME/ARNE/CAGE2	Douglas-fir/pinemat manzanita/elk sedge
		PSME/CAGE2	Douglas-fir/elk sedge
		PSME/CARU*	Douglas-fir/pinegrass
		PSME/CELE3/CAGE2	Douglas-fir/mountain mahogany/elk sedge
		PSME/PHMA5	Douglas-fir/mallow ninebark
		PSME/SPBE2	Douglas-fir/birchleaf spiraea
		PSME/SYAL*	Douglas-fir/common snowberry
		PSME/SYOR2*	Douglas-fir/mountain snowberry
		PSME/SYOR2/CAGE2	Douglas-fir/mountain snowberry/elk sedge
		PSME/VAME*	Douglas-fir/big huckleberry
		PSME-PIPO-JUOC/FEID	Douglas-fir-ponderosa pine-western juniper/Idaho fescue
	Hot moist	PIPO/ARAR8	ponderosa pine/low sagebrush
	Hot dry	PIPO/AGSP*	ponderosa pine/bluebunch wheatgrass
		PIPO/ARTRV/CAGE2	ponderosa pine/mountain big sagebrush/elk sedge
		PIPO/ARTRV/FEID-AGSP	ponderosa pine/mountain big sagebrush/Idaho fescue-bluebunch wheatgrass
		PIPO/CELE3/FEID-AGSP	ponderosa pine/mountain mahogany/Idaho fescue-bluebunch wheatgrass
		PIPO/CELE3/PONEW	ponderosa pine/mountain mahogany/Wheeler's bluegrass
		PIPO/FEID*	ponderosa pine/Idaho fescue
		PIPO/PERA4	ponderosa pine/squaw apple
		PIPO/PUTR2/AGSP	ponderosa pine/bitterbrush/bluebunch wheatgrass
		PIPO/PUTR2/AGSP-POSA12	ponderosa pine/bitterbrush/bluebunch wheatgrass-Sandberg's bluegrass
		PIPO/PUTR2/FEID-AGSP	ponderosa pine/bitterbrush/Idaho fescue-bluebunch wheatgrass
		PIPO/RHGL	ponderosa pine/smooth sumac
		PIPO-JUOC/CELE3-SYOR2	ponderosa pine-western juniper/mountain mahogany-mountain snowberry

Table 2–Potential vegetation groups (PVG), plant association groups (PAG), and potential vegetation type (PVT) codes and common names for upland physiognomic classes (continued)

PVG	PAG	PVT code (PLANTS code)	PVT common name
Moist upland woodland	Hot moist	JUOC/ARTRV/FEID-AGSP	western juniper/mountain big sagebrush/Idaho fescue-bluebunch wheatgrass
		JUOC/CELE3/CAGE2	western juniper/mountain mahogany/elk sedge
		JUOC/CELE3/FEID-AGSP	western juniper/mountain mahogany/Idaho fescue-bluebunch wheatgrass
		JUOC/FEID-AGSP	western juniper/Idaho fescue-bluebunch wheatgrass
		JUOC/PUTR2/FEID-AGSP	western juniper/bitterbrush/Idaho fescue-bluebunch wheatgrass
Dry upland woodland	Hot dry	JUOC/AGSP	western juniper/bluebunch wheatgrass
		JUOC/ARAR8	western juniper/low sagebrush
		JUOC/ARAR8/FEID	western juniper/low sagebrush/Idaho fescue
		JUOC/ARRI2*	western juniper/stiff sagebrush
Cold upland shrub	Cold very moist	ALSI3	Sitka alder snow slides
	Cold moist	ARTRV/CAGE2	mountain big sagebrush/elk sedge
		ARTRV/CAHO5	mountain big sagebrush/Hood's sedge
		ARTRV/FEVI	mountain big sagebrush/green fescue
	Cool dry	ARTRV/ERFL4-PHLOX	mountain big sagebrush/golden buckwheat-phlox
		ARTRV/LINU4	mountain big sagebrush/linanthus
		ARTRV/STOC2	mountain big sagebrush/western needlegrass
	Cool moist	POFR4	shrubby cinquefoil
Moist upland shrub	Warm moist	ARAR8/FEID-AGSP	low sagebrush/Idaho fescue-bluebunch wheatgrass
		ARTRV/BRCA5	mountain big sagebrush/mountain brome
		ARTRV/CAGE2 (MONTANE)	mountain big sagebrush/elk sedge (montane)
		ARTRV/ELCI2	mountain big sagebrush/basin wildrye
		ARTRV/FEID-AGSP	mountain big sagebrush/Idaho fescue-bluebunch wheatgrass
		ARTRV/FEID-KOCR	mountain big sagebrush/Idaho fescue-prairie junegrass
		ARTRV-PERA4	mountain big sagebrush-squaw apple
		ARTRV-SYOR2	mountain big sagebrush-mountain snowberry
		ARTRV-SYOR2/BRCA5	mountain big sagebrush-mountain snowberry/mountain brome
		CELE3/CAGE2*	mountain mahogany/elk sedge
		CELE3/FEID-AGSP	mountain mahogany/Idaho fescue-bluebunch wheatgrass
		CELE3-PUTR2/AGSP	mountain mahogany-bitterbrush/bluebunch wheatgrass
		CEVE	snowbrush ceanothus
		JUCO6	mountain juniper
		PHMA5-SYAL*	mallow ninebark-common snowberry
		POFR4/FEID	shrubby cinquefoil/Idaho fescue
		PREM	bitter cherry
		PUTR2/FEID-AGSP	bitterbrush/Idaho fescue-bluebunch wheatgrass
		PUTR2-ARTRV/FEID	bitterbrush-mountain big sagebrush/Idaho fescue
		PUTR2-ARTRV/FEID-AGSP	bitterbrush-mountain big sagebrush/Idaho fescue-bluebunch wheatgrass
		SYAL	common snowberry
		SYAL/FEID-AGSP-LUSE4	common snowberry/Idaho fescue-bluebunch wheatgrass-silky lupine
		SYAL/FEID-KOCR	common snowberry/Idaho fescue-prairie junegrass
		SYAL-ROSA5	common snowberry-rose
		SYOR2	mountain snowberry

Table 2–Potential vegetation groups (PVG), plant association groups (PAG), and potential vegetation type (PVT) codes and common names for upland physiognomic classes (continued)

PVG	PAG	PVT code (PLANTS code)	PVT common name
Moist upland shrub	Hot very moist	PHLE4 (TALUS)	syringa-bordered talus strips
	Hot moist	ARTRV-PUTR2/FEID	mountain big sagebrush-bitterbrush/Idaho fescue
		CERE2/AGSP	netleaf hackberry/bluebunch wheatgrass
		PERA4-SYOR2	squaw apple-mountain snowberry
		PUTR2/AGSP	bitterbrush/bluebunch wheatgrass
Dry upland shrub	Warm dry	ARAR8/AGSP	low sagebrush/bluebunch wheatgrass
		ARAR8/POSA12	low sagebrush/Sandberg's bluegrass
		ARRI2/PEGA	stiff sagebrush/Gairdner's penstemon
		ARRI2/POSA12 (SCAB)	stiff sagebrush/Sandberg's bluegrass (scabland)
		ARTR4/POSA12-DAUN	threetip sagebrush/Sandberg's bluegrass-onespike oatgrass
		ARTRV/AGSP-POSA12	mountain big sagebrush/bluebunch wheatgrass-Sandberg's bluegrass
		BERE/AGSP-APAN2	creeping Oregongrape/bluebunch wheatgrass-spreading dogbane
		CELE3	mountain mahogany
		CELE3/AGSP	mountain mahogany/bluebunch wheatgrass
		CELE3/PONEW	mountain mahogany/Wheeler's bluegrass
		PUTR2/ERDO	bitterbrush/Douglas' buckwheat
	Hot dry	GLSPA/AGSP	spiny greasebush/bluebunch wheatgrass
		RHGL/AGSP	smooth sumac/bluebunch wheatgrass
Cold upland herb	Cold moist	FEID (ALPINE)	Idaho fescue (alpine)
		FEVI	green fescue
		FEVI-AGCA2	green fescue-bearded wheatgrass
		FEVI-CAHO5	green fescue-Hood's sedge
		FEVI-CARO5	green fescue-Ross' sedge
		FEVI-CASC12	green fescue-Holm's Rocky Mountain sedge
		FEVI-LICA2	green fescue-Canby's lovageCold dry
		FEVI-LULA3	green fescue-spurred lupine
		FEVI-PENST	green fescue-penstemon
		FEVI-STOC2	green fescue-western needlegrass
		POPH (CORNICES)	alpine fleeceflower (cornices)
		POPH-FEVI	alpine fleeceflower-green fescue
	Cold dry	CAGE2-CARU	elk sedge-pinegrass
		CAGE2-FEID	elk sedge-Idaho fescue
		CAGE2-JUPA	elk sedge-Parry's rush
		CAGE2-PHAU3	elk sedge-desert phlox
		CAGE2-POCU	elk sedge-Cusick's bluegrass
		CAGE2-STOC2	elk sedge-western needlegrass
		CAREX-STOC2	alpine sedges-western needlegrass
		FELLFIELD	fellfield
		FESC-FEID	rough fescue-Idaho fescue
		FEVI-JUPA	green fescue-Parry's rush
		GRUS	grus

Table 2–Potential vegetation groups (PVG), plant association groups (PAG), and potential vegetation type (PVT) codes and common names for upland physiognomic classes (continued)

PVG	PAG	PVT code (PLANTS code)	PVT common name
Cold upland herb	Cold dry	JUPA-AGGL	Parry's rush-pale agoseris
		PHLOX-CYTEF	phlox-cymopterus
		PHLOX-IVGO	phlox-Ivesia
		ROCK OUTCROP	rock outcrop
		SCREE	scree
		TURF	turf
	Cool moist	CAHO5	Hood's sedge
		CAHO5-BRCA5*	Hood's sedge-mountain brome
		CAHO5-CAGE2	Hood's sedge-elk sedge
		FEID-AGSP-FRALC2	Idaho fescue-bluebunch wheatgrass-Cusick's frasera
		FEID-GETR	Idaho fescue-red avens
		FEID-KOCR*	Idaho fescue-prairie junegrass
		FEID-PESP2	Idaho fescue-Wallowa penstemon
		LEPY2-MAGL2	pygmy Lewisia-cluster tarweed
		LINU4-ARLO6	Nuttall's linanthus-longleaf arnica
		POPR (DEGEN BENCH)	Kentucky bluegrass (degenerated bench)
		PTAQ-CAHO5	bracken fern-Hood's sedge
		RUOC2-MAGL2	western coneflower-cluster tarweed
		STOC2	western needlegrass
	Cool dry	CAHO5-POGL9	Hood's sedge-sticky cinquefoil
		ERFL4-PECO	golden buckwheat-coiled lousewort
		LINU4-ARLU	linanthus-mountain mugwort
		LINU4-CYTEF	linanthus-cymopterus
		MOOD	mountain balm
		POPH-AGUR-LINU4	alpine fleeceflower-horsemint-linanthus
		POPH-CAGE2-LINU4	alpine fleeceflower-elk sedge-linanthus
		POPH-CARU-CAGE2	alpine fleeceflower-pinegrass-elk sedge
Moist upland herb	Warm very moist	CACU2 (SEEP)	Cusick's camas (seep)
		FEID-DAIN-CAPE7	Idaho fescue-timber oatgrass-Liddon's sedge
	Warm moist	AGSP-BRCA5	bluebunch wheatgrass-mountain brome
		FEID-AGSP*	Idaho fescue-bluebunch wheatgrass
		FEID-AGSP-BASA3	Idaho fescue-bluebunch wheatgrass-arrowleaf balsamroot
		FEID-AGSP-LUPIN	Idaho fescue-bluebunch wheatgrass-lupine
		FEID-AGSP-PHCO10	Idaho fescue-bluebunch wheatgrass-Snake River phlox
		FEID-AGSP-PHLOX	Idaho fescue-bluebunch wheatgrass-phlox
		FEID-CAGE2	Idaho fescue-elk sedge
		FEID-CAHO5	Idaho fescue-Hood's sedge
		FEID-KOCR (LOW)	Idaho fescue-prairie junegrass (low elevation)
	Hot very moist	ELCI2	basin wildrye
	Hot moist	DAUN-LOLE2	onespike oatgrass-slenderfruit lomatium

Table 2–Potential vegetation groups (PVG), plant association groups (PAG), and potential vegetation type (PVT) codes and common names for upland physiognomic classes (continued)

PVG	PAG	PVT code (PLANTS code)	PVT common name
Dry upland herb	Warm dry	FEID-AGSP-CYTEF	Idaho fescue-bluebunch wheatgrass-cymopterus
		FEID-AGSP-PONEW	Idaho fescue-bluebunch wheatgrass-Wheeler's bluegrass
		FEID-DAUN	Idaho fescue-onespike oatgrass
		MEBU-STOC2	oniongrass-western needlegrass
		POSA12-SELA	Sandberg's bluegrass-lanceleaf stonecrop
		STOC2-SIHY (ALPINE)	western needlegrass-squirreltail (alpine)
	Hot dry	AGSP-CYTEF	bluebunch wheatgrass-cymopterus
		AGSP-ERHE2	bluebunch wheatgrass-Wyeth's buckwheat
		AGSP-ERUM	bluebunch wheatgrass-sulphurflower buckwheat
		AGSP-POSA12*	bluebunch wheatgrass-Sandberg's bluegrass
		AGSP-POSA12-APAN2	bluebunch wheatgrass-Sandberg's bluegrass-spreading dogbane
		AGSP-POSA12-ASCU5	bluebunch wheatgrass-Sandberg's bluegrass-Cusick's milkvetch
		AGSP-POSA12-ASRE5	bluebunch wheatgrass-Sandberg's bluegrass-Blue Mountain milkvetch
		AGSP-POSA12-BASA3	bluebunch wheatgrass-Sandberg's bluegrass-arrowleaf balsamroot
		AGSP-POSA12-DAUN	bluebunch wheatgrass-Sandberg's bluegrass-onespike oatgrass
		AGSP-POSA12-ERHE2	bluebunch wheatgrass-Sandberg's bluegrass-creamy buckwheat
		AGSP-POSA12-ERPU2	bluebunch wheatgrass-Sandberg's bluegrass-shaggy fleabane
		AGSP-POSA12-LUPIN	bluebunch wheatgrass-Sandberg's bluegrass-lupine
		AGSP-POSA12-OPPO	bluebunch wheatgrass-Sandberg's bluegrass-pricklypear
		AGSP-POSA12-PHCO10	bluebunch wheatgrass-Sandberg's bluegrass-Snake River phlox
		AGSP-POSA12-SCAN3	bluebunch wheatgrass-Sandberg's bluegrass-narrowleaf skullcap
		AGSP-POSA12-TRMA3	bluebunch wheatgrass-Sandberg's bluegrass-bighead clover
		AGSP-SPCR-ARLO3	bluebunch wheatgrass-sand dropseed-red threeawn
		ERDO-POSA12	Douglas' buckwheat-Sandberg's bluegrass
		ERIOG/PHOR2	buckwheat/Oregon bladderpod
		ERST4-POSA12	strict buckwheat/Sandberg's bluegrass
		ERUM (RIDGE)	sulphurflower (ridge)
		LECOW2 (RIM)	Wallowa Lewisia (rim)
		POBU-MAGL2	bulbous bluegrass-cluster tarweed
		POSA12-DAUN	Sandberg's bluegrass-onespike oatgrass
		SPCR (TERRACE)	sand dropseed (terrace)

* The PVT has been described for more than one of the Blue Mountains potential vegetation classifications (Crowe and Clausnitzer 1997, Johnson 2004, Johnson and Clausnitzer 1992, Johnson and Simon 1987, Johnson and Swanson 2005, and Wells 2006) and is listed more than once in appendix tables 8 and 9 (each listing has a different ecoclass code).

Table 3—A 12-cell matrix of temperature and soil moisture categories

Temperature	Soil moisture (SM)		
	High	**Moderate**	**Low**
Cold	Cold high SM	Cold moderate SM	Cold low SM
Cool	Cool high SM	Cool moderate SM	Cool low SM
Warm	Warm high SM	Warm moderate SM	Warm low SM
Hot	Hot high SM	Hot moderate SM	Hot low SM

A 4 by 3 temperature-moisture matrix like the one shown here was used for the three physiognomic classes included in table 4: riparian forest, riparian shrub, and riparian herb. The fine-scale potential vegetation types occurring in a riparian physiognomic class were assigned to one, and only one, of the class's matrix cells. Individual matrix cells (cool low SM, etc.) are used as plant association groups in the midscale portion of the potential vegetation hierarchy (fig. 2).

Assignment of riparian PVTs to physiognomic temperature-moisture matrices is presented for the three riparian forest physiognomic classes (table 4).

Potential Vegetation Groups

Potential vegetation information was used extensively during the interior Columbia River basin scientific assessment (Quigley and Arbelbide 1997, Quigley et al. 1996). When analyzing such a large area, however, it was found that the level of detail associated with PAGs (e.g., temperature-moisture matrix cells) was at too fine a scale for examining trends across a large assessment area containing portions of seven Western States. Therefore, PAGs were aggregated into a higher level taxonomic unit called potential vegetation groups (PVGs) (Jensen et al. 1997).

For the Blue Mountains section, PVGs are the middle level of the midscale portion of the PV hierarchy (fig. 2). Two or three PVGs were established for each of the seven physiognomic classes. Potential vegetation groups are named for a predominant or controlling temperature or moisture relationship (table 5).

The midscale portion of the PV hierarchy is described in tables 2 and 4; each table shows fine-scale PVTs organized by physiognomic class, PVT aggregations into PAGs (PVTs grouped into temperature-moisture cells), and PAG aggregations into PVGs.

Summary statistics for both portions of the PV hierarchy (e.g., fine-scale and midscale) are presented in table 6.

The appendix shows how 507 fine-scale PVTs described for the Blue Moun-

Potential vegetation groups are named for a predominant or controlling temperature or moisture relationship.

Table 4–Potential vegetation groups (PVG), plant association groups (PAG), and potential vegetation type (PVT) codes and common names for riparian physiognomic classes

PVG	PAG	PVT code (PLANTS code)	PVT common name
Cold riparian forest	Cold high soil moisture (SM)	ABLA/ATFI	subalpine fir/ladyfern
		ABLA/CAAQ	subalpine fir/aquatic sedge
		ABLA/CADI6	subalpine fir/softleaf sedge
		ABLA/SETR	subalpine fir/arrowleaf groundsel
		ABLA/VAUL/CASC12	subalpine fir/bog blueberry/Holm's Rocky Mountain sedge
		ABLA-PIEN/LEGL (FLOODPLAIN)	subalpine fir/Engelmann spruce/Labrador tea (floodplain)
		PICO/CAAQ	lodgepole pine/aquatic sedge
		PICO/CASC12	lodgepole pine/Holm's Rocky Mountain sedge
		PIEN/ATFI	Engelmann spruce/ladyfern
		PIEN/CADI6	Engelmann spruce/softleaf sedge
		PIEN/SETR	Engelmann spruce/arrowleaf groundsel
		PIEN-ABLA/CASC12	Engelmann spruce-subalpine fir/Holm's Rocky Mountain sedge
		PIEN-ABLA/SETR	Engelmann spruce-subalpine fir/arrowleaf groundsel
	Cold moderate SM	ABLA/CACA4	subalpine fir/bluejoint reedgrass
		ABLA/VAME (FLOODPLAIN)	subalpine fir/big huckleberry (floodplain)
		ABLA-PIEN/MEFE (FLOODPLAIN)	subalpine fir-Engelmann spruce (floodplain)
		PICO/ALIN2/MESIC FORB	lodgepole pine/mountain alder/mesic forb
		PICO/CACA4	lodgepole pine/bluejoint reedgrass
		PICO/CALA30	lodgepole pine/woolly sedge
		PICO/DECE	lodgepole pine/tufted hairgrass
		PIEN/CILA2	Engelmann spruce/drooping woodreed
		PIEN/COST4	Engelmann spruce/red osier dogwood
		PIEN/EQAR	Engelmann spruce/common horsetail
	Cold low SM	PICO/POPR	lodgepole pine/Kentucky bluegrass
		PIEN/BRVU	Engelmann spruce/Columbia brome
Warm riparian forest	Warm high SM	ABGR/ATFI	grand fir/ladyfern
		ABGR/CALA30	grand fir/woolly sedge
		ABGR/CRDO2/CADE9	grand fir/black hawthorn/Dewey's sedge
		ABGR/TABR2/LIBO3 (FLOODPLAIN)	grand fir/Pacific yew/twinflower (floodplain)
		ALRU2/ATFI	red alder/ladyfern
		POTR5/CAAQ	quaking aspen/aquatic sedge
	Warm moderate SM	ABGR/ACGL (FLOODPLAIN)	grand fir/Rocky Mountain maple (floodplain)
		ALRU2 (ALLUVIAL BAR)	red alder (alluvial bar)
		ALRU2/COST4	red alder/red osier dogwood
		ALRU2/PEFRP	red alder/sweet coltsfoot
		ALRU2/PHCA11	red alder/Pacific ninebark
		ALRU2/SYAL	red alder/common snowberry
		ALRU2/SYAL/CADE9	red alder/common snowberry/Dewey's sedge
		PIMO3/DECE	western white pine/tufted hairgrass
		POTR5/ALIN2-COST4	quaking aspen/mountain alder-red osier dogwood
		POTR5/ALIN2-SYAL	quaking aspen/mountain alder-common snowberry
		POTR5/CACA4	quaking aspen/bluejoint reedgrass
		POTR5/CALA30	quaking aspen/woolly sedge
		POTR5/MESIC FORB	quaking aspen/mesic forb
		POTR15/ACGL	black cottonwood/Rocky Mountain maple
		POTR15/ALIN2-COST4	black cottonwood/mountain alder-red osier dogwood
		PSME/ACGL-PHMA5 (FLOODPLAIN)	Douglas-fir/Rocky Mountain maple-ninebark (floodplain)
		PSME/TRCA	Douglas-fir/false bugbane

Table 4–Potential vegetation groups (PVG), plant association groups (PAG), and potential vegetation type (PVT) codes and common names for riparian physiognomic classes (continued)

PVG	PAG	PVT code (PLANTS code)	PVT common name
Warm riparian forest	Hot moderate SM	ALRH2/MESIC SHRUB	white alder/mesic shrub
		ALRH2/RUBUS	white alder/blackberry
		PIPO/CRDO2	ponderosa pine/black hawthorn
		POTR15/SALA5	black cottonwood/Pacific willow
		POTR5/SYAL	quaking aspen/common snowberry
		POTR15/SYAL*	black cottonwood/common snowberry
Low SM riparian forest	Warm low SM	ABGR/SYAL (FLOODPLAIN)	grand fir/common snowberry (floodplain)
		PSME/SYAL (FLOODPLAIN)	Douglas-fir/common snowberry (floodplain)
	Hot low SM	PIPO/POPR	ponderosa pine/Kentucky bluegrass
		PIPO/SYAL (FLOODPLAIN)	ponderosa pine/common snowberry (floodplain)
		POTR5/POPR	quaking aspen/Kentucky bluegrass
Cold riparian shrub	Cold high SM	KAMI/CANI2	alpine laurel/black alpine sedge
		SAAR27	arctic willow
		SABO2/CASC12	Booth's willow/Holm's Rocky Mountain sedge
		SABO2/CAVE6	Booth's willow/inflated sedge
		SACO2/CAPR5	undergreen willow/clustered field sedge
		SACO2/CASC12	undergreen willow/Holm's Rocky Mountain sedge
		SACO2/CAUT	undergreen willow/bladder sedge
		SADR/SETR	Drummond's willow/arrowleaf groundsel
		SAFA/ALVA	Farr's willow/Pacific onion
	Cold moderate SM	LEGL/CASC12	Labrador tea/Holm's Rocky Mountain sedge
		PHEM (MOUNDS)	pink mountainheath (mounds)
		POFR4-BEGL	shrubby cinquefoil-bog birch
	Cool high SM	SALIX/CAAQ	willow/aquatic sedge
	Cool moderate SM	SALIX/CACA4	willow/bluejoint reedgrass
Warm riparian shrub	Warm high SM	ALIN2/ATFI	mountain alder/ladyfern
		ALIN2/CAAM10	mountain alder/bigleaf sedge
		ALIN2/CAAQ	mountain alder/aquatic sedge
		ALIN2/CAUT	mountain alder/bladder sedge
		ALIN2/GLEL	mountain alder/tall mannagrass
		ALIN2/SCMI2	mountain alder/smallfruit bulrush
		ALSI3/ATFI	Sitka alder/ladyfern
		ALSI3/CILA2	Sitka alder/drooping woodreed
		BEOC2/WET SEDGE	water birch/wet sedge
		COST4/ATFI	red osier dogwood/ladyfern
		COST4/SAAR13	Red osier dogwood/brook saxifrage
		RIBES/CILA2	currants/drooping woodreed
		RIBES/GLEL	currants/tall mannagrass
		SAEA-SATW/CAAQ	Eastwood willow-Tweedy willow/aquatic sedge
		SALIX/CAUT	willow/bladder sedge
		SASI2/EQAR	Sitka willow/common horsetail

Table 4—Potential vegetation groups (PVG), plant association groups (PAG), and potential vegetation type (PVT) codes and common names for riparian physiognomic classes (continued)

PVG	PAG	PVT code (PLANTS code)	PVT common name
Warm riparian shrubs	Warm moderate SM	ALIN2/CACA4	mountain alder/bluejoint reedgrass
		ALIN2/CADE9	mountain alder/Dewey's sedge
		ALIN2/CALA30	mountain alder/woolly sedge
		ALIN2/CALEL	mountain alder/densely tufted sedge
		ALIN2/EQAR	mountain alder/common horsetail
		ALIN2/GYDR	mountain alder/oakfern
		ALIN2/HELA4	mountain alder/common cowparsnip
		ALIN2-COST4/MESIC FORB	mountain alder-red osier dogwood/mesic forb
		ALIN2-RIBES/MESIC FORB	mountain alder-currants/mesic forb
		ALSI3/MESIC FORB	Sitka alder/mesic forb
		BEOC2/MESIC FORB	water birch/mesic forb
		BEOC2/PHAR3	water birch/reed canarygrass
		COST4	red osier dogwood
		LOIN5/ATFI	twinberry honeysuckle/ladyfern
		POFR4/DECE	shrubby cinquefoil/tufted hairgrass
		RHAL/MESIC FORB	alderleaf buckthorn/mesic forb
		RIBES/MESIC FORB	currants/mesic forb
		SAEX	coyote willow
		SALE/MESIC FORB	Lemmon's willow/mesic forb
		SALIX/CALA30	willow/woolly sedge
		SALIX/MESIC FORB	willow/mesic forb
	Hot moderate SM	ARCA13/DECE	silver sagebrush/tufted hairgrass
		RUDI2	Himalayan blackberry
		RUPA	thimbleberry
		SARI2	rigid willow
		SYAL (FLOODPLAIN)	common snowberry (floodplain)
Low SM riparian shrub	Warm low SM	ALIN2/CALU7	mountain alder/woodrush sedge
		ALIN2/POPR	mountain alder/Kentucky bluegrass
		ALIN2-SYAL	mountain alder-common snowberry
		PHCA11	Pacific ninebark
		POFR4/POPR	shrubby cinquefoil/Kentucky bluegrass
		SALIX/POPR	willow/Kentucky bluegrass
		SASC/ELGL	Scouler's willow/blue wildrye
	Hot low SM	ACGL	Rocky Mountain maple
		AMAL2	western serviceberry
		ARCA13/POCU3	silver sagebrush/Cusick's bluegrass
		ARCA13/POPR	silver sagebrush/Kentucky bluegrass
		ARTRV/POCU3	mountain big sagebrush/Cusick's bluegrass
		CERE2/BROMU	netleaf hackberry/brome
		CRDO2/MESIC FORB	black hawthorn/mesic forb
		PHLE4/MESIC FORB	Lewis' mockorange/mesic forb
		RUBA	Barton's raspberry

Table 4–Potential vegetation groups (PVG), plant association groups (PAG), and potential vegetation type (PVT) codes and common names for riparian physiognomic classes (continued)

PVG	PAG	PVT code (PLANTS code)	PVT common name
Cold riparian herb	Cold high SM	ALVA	Pacific onion
		ALVA-CASC12	Pacific onion-Holm's Rocky Mountain sedge
		CAEU2	widefruit sedge
		CALA13	smoothstemmed sedge
		CALE9	Sierra hare sedge
		CALI7	mud sedge
		CALU7	woodrush sedge
		CAPR5	clustered field sedge
		CASC10-SAAR13	northern singlespike sedge-brook saxifrage
		CASC12	Holm's Rocky Mountain sedge
		CILA2	drooping woodreed
		ELBE	delicate spikerush
		ELPA6	fewflowered spikerush
		SPAN2	narrowleaf bur-reed
	Cold moderate SM	CANI2	black alpine sedge
	Cool high SM	CAAQ	aquatic sedge
		CAUT	bladder sedge
		CAVE6	inflated sedge
		NUPO2	Rocky Mountain pondlily
		SETR-MILE2	arrowleaf groundsel-purple monkeyflower
	Cool moderate SM	CACA4	bluejoint reedgrass
		DECE	tufted hairgrass
Warm riparian herb	Warm high SM	ADPE	maidenhair fern
		CAAM10	bigleaf sedge
		CACU5	Cusick's sedge
		CALA11	slender sedge
		CASI2	shortbeaked sedge
		CAST5	sawbeak sedge
		GLEL	tall mannagrass
		METR3	buckbean
		PUPA3	weak alkaligrass
		SAAR13	brook saxifrage
		SCMI2	smallfruit bulrush
		SETR	arrowleaf groundsel
		VEAM2	American speedwell

Table 4—Potential vegetation groups (PVG), plant association groups (PAG), and potential vegetation type (PVT) codes and common names for riparian physiognomic classes (continued)

PVG	PAG	PVT code (PLANTS code)	PVT common name
Warm riparian herb	Warm moderate SM	CACA11	silvery sedge
		CAJO	Jones' sedge
		CALA30	woolly sedge
		CALE8	lakeshore sedge
		CAMI7	smallwing sedge
		CAMU7	star sedge
		CANE2	Nebraska sedge
		CASU6	brown sedge
		EQAR	common horsetail
		HELA4-ELGL	common cowparsnip/blue wildrye
		JUBA	Baltic rush
		RUOC2	western coneflower
		VERAT*	false hellebore
	Hot high SM	CANU5	torrent sedge
		ELPA3	creeping spikerush
		TYLA	common cattail
	Hot moderate SM	CASH	Sheldon's sedge
Low SM riparian herb	Warm low SM	AGDI	thin bentgrass
		ALPR3	meadow foxtail
		ARLU	white sagebrush
		POPR (DRY MEADOW)	Kentucky bluegrass (dry meadow)

Note that PVT codes followed by an asterisk denote instances where a PVT has been described for more than one of the Blue Mountains potential vegetation classifications (Crowe and Clausnitzer 1997, Johnson 2004, Johnson and Clausnitzer 1992, Johnson and Simon 1987, Johnson and Swanson 2005, and Wells 2006) and are listed more than once in appendix tables 8 and 9 (each listing has a different ecoclass code).

Table 5–Potential vegetation groups associated with seven physiognomic classes for the Blue Mountains section

Physiognomic class						
Upland forest	**Upland shrub**	**Upland herb**	**Upland woodland**	**Riparian forest**	**Riparian shrub**	**Riparian herb**
Cold upland forest	Cold upland shrub	Cold upland herb		Cold riparian forest	Cold riparian shrub	Cold riparian herb
Moist upland forest	Moist upland shrub	Moist upland herb	Moist upland woodland	Warm riparian forest	Warm riparian shrub	Warm riparian herb
Dry upland forest	Dry upland shrub	Dry upland herb	Dry upland woodland	Low SM riparian forest	Low SM riparian shrub	Low SM riparian herb

SM = soil moisture.

Table 6—Summary statistics pertaining to the mid- and fine-scale portions of the potential vegetation hierarchy for the Blue Mountains section

Potential vegetation unit	Potential units[a]	Actual units[b]
Midscale hierarchical units		
Physiognomic classes	8	7
Potential vegetation groups	21	20
Plant association groups	100	58
Fine-scale hierarchical units		
Series	NA	[d]
Potential vegetation types[c]:	NA	507
Phases	NA	[d]

[a] Total number of possible units when based on the classification framework used to develop the midscale portion of the potential vegetation hierarchy (see fig. 2); NA (not applicable) is shown for the fine-scale portion of the hierarchy because at that scale, the number of potential units is a function of vegetation occurrence (i.e., vegetation habitat as determined by biophysical environments) rather than the classification framework itself.

[b] The number of hierarchical units actually established for the Blue Mountains section. When the "actual units" value is less than the "potential units" value, it means that one or more framework entities (cells in a temperature-moisture matrix, for example) were empty or not used for the Blue Mountains section.

[c] In the context of this report, "potential vegetation types" refers to three taxonomic units described in fine-scale potential vegetation classifications for the Blue Mountains section (plant associations, plant community types, and plant communities as described in Crowe and Clausnitzer 1997, Johnson 2004, Johnson and Clausnitzer 1992, Johnson and Simon 1987, Johnson and Swanson 2005, and Wells 2006).

[d] Neither series nor phases were used for the fine-scale portion of the Blue Mountains potential vegetation hierarchy.

tains section (Crowe and Clausnitzer 1997, Johnson 2004, Johnson and Clausnitzer 1992, Johnson and Simon 1987, Johnson and Swanson 2005, Wells 2006) were assigned to midscale hierarchical units (PAGs and PVGs). Appendix table 8 organizes this information by PVT code; appendix table 9 organizes it by ecoclass code (Hall 1998, as supplemented).

A step-down process was used to develop the physiognomic classes, PVGs and PAGs.

Step-Down Process for Developing Midscale Hierarchical Units

The interior Columbia River basin scientific assessment area contains all or part of 7 terrestrial ecological provinces and 23 sections (Jensen et al. 1997); the process described below was used to step the broad-scale PV framework down to the hierarchical level of a single section (section M332G, the "Blue Mountains," in province M332, middle Rocky Mountain steppe–coniferous forest–alpine meadow) (Bailey 1995, 1998; Cleland et al. 1997; McNab and Avers 1994).

The step-down process was used to develop the physiognomic classes, PVGs and PAGs described in the previous section and shown in tables 2 and 4.

1. During preparation of an ecosystem components assessment for the interior Columbia River basin assessment area (Quigley and Arbelbide 1997), each upland PVT described for the Blue Mountains section was assigned to one of four temperature-moisture matrices: upland forest, upland woodland, upland shrub, and upland herb (Reid et al. 1995). The matrices were selected to reflect vegetation physiognomy or life form differences.

2. A Umatilla National Forest PV working group reviewed the upland temperature-moisture matrices developed for the Blue Mountains section and decided to adopt the matrix cells as PAGs (Powell 1998).

3. Eventually, all three Blue Mountains national forests (Malheur, Umatilla, and Wallowa-Whitman) agreed to adopt the temperature-moisture matrix approach as a PV framework for meeting midscale assessment needs (USDA Forest Service 2002).

4. The three Blue Mountains national forests then decided how PAGs (temperature-moisture matrix cells) would be aggregated to form the middle level of the midscale portion of the PV hierarchy, PVGs.

5. A Blue Mountains PV working group made initial PVT assignments for the riparian matrices (forest, shrub, herb). For the interior Columbia River basin assessment effort, riparian PVTs had been assigned to a riparian PAG by using three criteria: membership in, or a linkage to, an upland matrix; physiognomy (life form); and riparian moisture phase (low, moderate, or high) (Manning and Engelking 1997). This approach was conceptually inconsistent

with how the upland matrices had been developed, so the Blue Mountains group decided to use the temperature categories adopted for the upland matrices (cold, cool, warm, hot) and to characterize moisture by using the riparian moisture phases (low, moderate, high) from the interior Columbia River basin riparian classification framework (Manning and Engelking 1997).

6. The final result of this process was two classification frameworks: a 4 by 4 temperature-moisture matrix used for each of four upland physiognomic classes (table 1), and a 4 by 3 temperature-soil moisture matrix used for each of three riparian physiognomic classes (table 3).

7. After the preliminary results of this process were documented (Powell 1998, USDA Forest Service 2002), the PV hierarchy began to be used for a variety of midscale purposes:

- The PAGs or PVGs are used as biophysical environments when conducting historical range of variability analyses comparing an area's existing and historical proportions of forest structure classes (Blackwood 1998, O'Hara et al. 1996, USDA Forest Service 1995).

- When revising the Land and Resource Management Plans for the Blue Mountains section, PAGs or PVGs were used for ecological stratification (USDA Forest Service 2002) during characterization of terrestrial and aquatic environments, and when modeling disturbance processes with the Vegetation Dynamics Development Tool (Beukema et al. 2003).

- The PAGs were used when deriving fire regimes (table 7) and biophysical settings, a prerequisite before characterizing an area's departure from its historical composition, structure, stand age, canopy cover, and patch configuration (Brown et al. 2004, Franklin and Agee 2003). The degree to which current vegetation conditions depart from historical conditions is referred to as the "fire regime condition class" descriptor (Hann et al. 2005, Morgan et al. 1996, Schmidt et al. 2002).

Concerns About Subjectivity

The matrix approach is based on a relative ranking of the temperature and moisture status represented by each fine-scale PVT. Because the rankings are relative, there may be a tendency to perceive overlap in the temperature-moisture relationships between PVTs, particularly for closely related types. For this reason, it may be difficult to decide which matrix cell is the best fit for types whose temperature or moisture relationships seem too broad to fit a single category.

A perception of temperature or moisture overlap is not surprising and occurs

Table 7–Relationship between plant association groups and fire regimes for the Blue Mountains section

Plant association group[a]	Fire regime[b]
Cold dry UF	3, 4
Cold dry UH	5
Cold high SM RF	4
Cold high SM RH	4
Cold high SM RS	4
Cold low SM RF	4
Cold moderate SM RF	4
Cold moist UF	4
Cold moist UH	4
Cold moist US	4
Cold very moist US	5
Cool dry UF	3, 4
Cool dry UH	4
Cool dry US	3
Cool moderate SM RH	4
Cool high SM RH	4
Cool moist UF	3, 4
Cool moist UH	2
Cool moist US	4
Cool very moist UF	4
Cool wet UF	4
Hot dry UF	1
Hot dry UH	2
Hot dry US	2
Hot dry UW	3
Hot high SM RH	4
Hot low SM RF	1
Hot low SM RS	1
Hot moderate SM RF	1
Hot moderate SM RH	3
Hot moderate SM RS	3
Hot moist UF	1
Hot moist UH	3
Hot moist US	3
Hot moist UW	3
Hot very moist UH	2
Hot very moist US	2
Warm dry UF	1
Warm dry UH	2
Warm dry US	2
Warm high SM RF	4
Warm high SM RH	4
Warm high SM RS	4
Warm low SM RF	1
Warm low SM RH	2
Warm low SM RS	4

Table 7–Relationship between plant association groups and fire regimes for the Blue Mountains section (continued)

Plant association group[a]	Fire regime[b]
Warm moderate SM RF	4
Warm moderate SM RH	4
Warm moderate SM RS	4
Warm moist UF	3
Warm moist UH	2
Warm moist US	2, 3
Warm very moist UF	3
Warm very moist UH	2

[a] Plant association group is the lowest level of the midscale portion of the potential vegetation hierarchy (fig. 2). Plant association group composition is described in tables 2 and 4.

[b] Fire regimes characterize the historical fire frequency and severity under which plant communities evolved (Franklin and Agee 2003, Morgan et al. 1996). Fire regimes, which are classified into five categories (Schmidt et al. 2002), are defined in the glossary.

frequently with ecological classification systems involving some element of interpretation or subjectivity. In some instances, the temperature or moisture overlap may be ecologically valid, in which case the zone of overlap can be thought of as an ecotone.

In many instances, however, perceived overlap in temperature or moisture relationships reflects differences of opinion about which portion of the environmental gradient is represented by a particular PVT (and its diagnostic indicator plants). For example, one practitioner might believe that the PSME/HODI plant association should be assigned to the "warm dry" temperature-moisture matrix cell, whereas another believes it best fits the "warm moist" cell.

Practitioners have different ecological experience and education, and these differences influence their perceptions about the temperature and moisture status of PVTs. This means that some difference of opinion about the environmental indicator status of PVTs is expected.

Even though the classification framework described in this report relies on interpretation (including some element of subjectivity), we believe the temperature-moisture matrix approach best reflects our current understanding of environmental gradients while also providing a conceptually sound process for establishing midscale taxonomic units of PV.

Glossary

abiotic—Nonliving components of the environment that are not currently part of living organisms, such as soils, rocks, water, air, light, and nutrients (Dunster and Dunster 1996).

aquatic—Waters of the United States, including wetlands, that serve as habitat for interrelated and interacting communities and populations of plants and animals (Maxwell et al. 1995).

biophysical environment—Landscape-level unit of vegetation composition and structure, with its associated environmental gradients and processes of change (Quigley and Arbelbide 1997).

biotic—Any living component of an ecosystem, including plants and animals and other organisms (Dunster and Dunster 1996); an entity distinct from abiotic physical and chemical components (Allaby 1998).

classification—The process of grouping similar entities together into named types or classes based on shared characteristics, or the grouping of similar types according to criteria that are considered significant for this purpose (Winthers et al. 2005).

climax—The culminating seral stage in plant succession for any given site where, in the absence of high-severity disturbances, the vegetation has reached a highly stable condition and undergoes change very slowly (Dunster and Dunster 1996). A self-replacing community that is relatively stable over several generations of the dominant plant species, or very persistent in comparison to other seral stages (Kimmins 1997).

coniferous—Trees bearing cones and commonly having needle-shaped leaves usually retained throughout the year; conifers are adapted to moisture deficiency caused by frozen ground or soils that are not moisture retentive (Bailey 1998).

ecological amplitude—The degree to which an organism can tolerate variations in environmental conditions (Dunster and Dunster 1996).

ecological type—A category of land or water having a unique and mappable combination of biotic and abiotic elements differing from other ecological types in its ability to produce vegetation and respond to management practices (Maxwell et al. 1995, Winthers et al. 2005).

ecological unit—A mapped terrestrial or aquatic unit comprising one or more ecological types, and designed to identify land and water areas at different levels of resolution (Maxwell et al. 1995). Map units designed to identify land and water areas at different levels of resolution based on similar capabilities and potentials for response to management and natural disturbance (Winthers et al. 2005).

ecology—The science studying the relationships among living things and their environment (Botkin 1990). This term was first coined in 1866 by Ernst Haeckel (Stauffer 1957). The major theme throughout the history of ecology and the concepts forming its foundation has been the interdependence of living things. An awareness, more philosophical than purely scientific, of this quality is what has generally been meant by an "ecological point of view" (Worster 1996).

ecosystem—A set of interacting species and their local, nonbiological environment, functioning together to sustain life (Botkin 1990). A.G. Tansley first used this term in 1935 to describe a discrete unit consisting of living and nonliving components, interacting to form a stable system (Tansley 1935).

existing vegetation—The plant cover, or floristic composition and vegetation structure, occurring at a given location at the current time (Winthers et al. 2005).

fire regime—A characterization of the historical combination of fire frequency and fire severity under which plant communities evolved and were maintained (Schmidt et al. 2002). Five fire regimes are currently recognized:

> **fire regime 1 (I):** 0- to 35-year fire frequency; low fire severity on dominant overstory vegetation.
>
> **fire regime 2 (II):** 0- to 35-year fire frequency; stand-replacement fire severity on dominant overstory vegetation.
>
> **fire regime 3 (III):** 35- to 100+ year fire frequency; mixed fire severity on dominant overstory vegetation.
>
> **fire regime 4 (IV):** 35- to 100+ year fire frequency; stand-replacement fire severity on dominant overstory vegetation.
>
> **fire regime 5 (V):** 200+ year fire frequency; stand-replacement fire severity on dominant overstory vegetation.

forb—Any broad-leaved, herbaceous plant other than grasses, sedges, and rushes (Helms 1998).

forb land—Land areas of sufficient size to be delineated as a mapping unit where the predominant vegetation life form consists of forbs.

forest—An ecosystem characterized by more or less dense and extensive tree cover, often consisting of stands varying in characteristics such as species composition, structure, age class and associated processes, and commonly including meadows, streams, fish, and wildlife (Helms 1998).

forest land—Land areas of sufficient size to be delineated as a mapping unit and at least 10 percent stocked by forest trees of any size, including land that formerly had such tree cover and will be naturally or artificially regenerated to trees (Helms 1998).

forest ecology—An understanding of the basic functional and physiological processes of forest ecosystems in order to sustain a wide range of forest conditions and values desired by society (Kimmins 1997).

graminoid—All grasses (Poaceae) and grass-like plants, including sedges (Cyperaceae) and rushes (Juncaceae) (Patterson et al. 1985).

grassland—Land areas of sufficient size to be delineated as a mapping unit where the predominant vegetation life form consists of graminoids.

habitat type—A basic ecological unit for classifying lands based on potential vegetation (Pfister and Arno 1980). It represents, collectively, all parts of the landscape that support, or have the capability to support, the same plant association (Alexander 1985). In effect, habitat types are mapping or land classification units; plant associations are their descriptors or taxonomic labels.

herb land—Land areas of sufficient size to be delineated as a mapping unit where the predominant vegetation life form consists of herbs (a combination of forbs and graminoids).

indicator plant—Plant species conveying information about the ecological nature of a site, such as the nitrogen content of its soil and soil alkalinity or acidity. These plant species have a sufficiently consistent association with a specific environmental condition or with other species such that their presence can be used to indicate or predict the environmental condition or the potential for the other species (Kimmins 1997).

life form—The structure, form, habits, and life history of an organism. In plants, characteristic life forms such as forest (trees), shrubs, and herbs (forbs/graminoids) are based on morphological features (physiognomy or predominant stature) that tend to be associated with different environments (Allaby 1998).

map unit—A collection of features defined and named the same in terms of a unifying theme; each map unit differs in some respect from all others within a geographic extent (Winthers et al. 2005).

phase—A taxonomic unit in a potential vegetation classification system; the lowest level in the fine-scale portion of the potential vegetation hierarchy (fig. 2). A phase represents minor environmental differences within a plant association or habitat type (Pfister and Arno 1980). A phase is named for an indicator plant species, such as the mallow ninebark phase of the grand fir/mountain maple habitat type in central Idaho (Steele et al. 1981).

physiognomy—The growth form and structure (habit) of vegetation in natural communities (Allaby 1998, Dunster and Dunster 1996). The characteristic feature or appearance of a plant community or vegetation (Winthers et al. 2005).

physiognomic class—Taxonomic categories or hierarchical units based on vegetation of similar physiognomy or life form, such as the upland forest, upland shrub and riparian herb physiognomic classes. Physiognomic class is the highest level in the midscale portion of the Blue Mountains potential vegetation hierarchy (fig. 2).

plant association—A taxonomic unit in a potential vegetation classification system (Pfister and Arno 1980). A plant association consists of plant communities with similar physiognomy (form and structure) and floristics; commonly it is a climax community (Allaby 1998). It is believed that (1) the individual species in the association are, to some extent, adapted to each other; (2) the association is made up of species that have similar environmental requirements; and (3) the association has some degree of integration (Kimmins 1997). Plant association is one of three taxonomic units included in the middle level of the fine-scale portion of the Blue Mountains potential vegetation hierarchy (this middle level is called potential vegetation type; fig. 2).

plant association group (PAG)—Groupings of plant associations (and other taxonomic units classified as potential vegetation types; fig. 2) representing similar ecological environments as characterized by temperature and moisture regimes. Plant association group is the lowest level in the midscale portion of the Blue Mountains potential vegetation hierarchy (fig. 2).

plant community—In a potential vegetation classification context, a plant community has no particular successional status. Generally, plant communities represent vegetation types with a restricted geographical distribution or they have such a small number of sample plots that it is not possible to infer their true successional status (Johnson and Clausnitzer 1992). Plant community is one of three taxonomic units included in the middle level of the fine-scale portion of the Blue Mountains potential vegetation hierarchy (this middle level is called potential vegetation type; fig. 2).

plant community type—In a potential vegetation classification context, plant community type is a taxonomic unit with no particular successional status implied (Dunster and Dunster 1996). Plant community type is one of three taxonomic units included in the middle level of the fine-scale portion of the Blue Mountains potential vegetation hierarchy (this middle level is called potential vegetation type; fig. 2).

plant succession—The process by which a series of different plant communities, and their associated animals and microbes, successively occupy and replace each other over time in a particular ecosystem or landscape location following a disturbance event (Kimmins 1997). Succession refers to the process of development of an ecosystem over time (Botkin 1990).

potential natural community (PNC)—The community of plants that would become established if all successional sequences were completed, without interference by people, under existing environmental conditions. Existing environmental conditions includes the current climate and eroded or damaged soils (Hall et al. 1995).

potential vegetation (PV)—The vegetation that would likely develop on a given site if all successional sequences were completed without human influence under present site conditions (USDA Forest Service 1996).

potential vegetation group (PVG)—An aggregation of plant association groups (PAGs) with similar environmental regimes and dominant plant species. Each aggregation (PVG) typically includes PAGs representing a predominant temperature or moisture influence (Powell 2000). Potential vegetation group is the middle level of the midscale portion of the Blue Mountains potential vegetation hierarchy (fig. 2).

potential vegetation type (PVT)—In the context of this report, a potential vegetation type is any taxonomic unit (except series) described in fine-scale potential vegetation classifications for the Blue Mountains section (e.g., Crowe and Clausnitzer 1997, Johnson 2004, Johnson and Clausnitzer 1992, Johnson and Simon 1987, Johnson and Swanson 2005, Wells 2006); PVT includes plant associations, plant community types, and plant communities. Potential vegetation type is the middle level of the fine-scale portion of the Blue Mountains potential vegetation hierarchy (fig. 2).

province—In the context of this report, a province is one of eight levels in the national hierarchical framework of terrestrial ecological units. Provinces are climatic subzones controlled primarily by such continental weather patterns as length of dry season and duration of cold temperatures. Provinces are also characterized by similar soil orders. Provinces are typically named by using a binomial system consisting of a geographical location and vegetation type: Bering tundra, California dry steppe, and middle Rocky Mountain steppe–coniferous forest–alpine meadow (Cleland et al. 1997, McNab and Avers 1994).

riparian—Related to, living near, or located in conjunction with a wetland; on the bank of a river or stream but also at the edge of a lake or tidewater. A riparian plant community significantly influences, and is significantly influenced by, the neighboring body of water (Helms 1998).

section—In the context of this report, a section is one of eight levels in the national hierarchical framework of terrestrial ecological units. Sections are broad areas of similar geomorphic process, stratigraphy, geologic origin, drainage networks, topography, and regional climate. Section names generally describe the predominant physiographic feature upon which the ecological unit delineation is based, such as Flint Hills, Appalachian piedmont, and Blue Mountains (Cleland et al. 1997, McNab and Avers 1994).

seral stage—The identifiable stages in the development of a sere, from an initial pioneer stage, through various early-seral and midseral stages, to late-seral, subclimax, and climax stages. The stages are characterized by different plant communities, different ages of the dominant vegetation, and by different microclimatic, soil, and forest conditions (Kimmins 1997). Hall et al. (1995) described four seral stages:

> **early seral**: clear dominance of seral species (such as western larch, ponderosa pine, and lodgepole pine); potential natural community (PNC) species are absent or present in very low numbers.

mid seral: PNC species are increasing in the forest composition as a result of their active colonization of the site; PNC species are approaching equal proportions with seral species.

late seral: PNC species are now dominant, although long-lived seral species (such as ponderosa pine and western larch) may still persist in the plant community.

potential natural community: the biotic community that one presumes would be established and maintained over time under present environmental conditions (climax); early-seral species are scarce or absent in the plant composition.

series—A taxonomic unit in a potential vegetation classification system. A series represents major environmental differences as reflected by a physiognomically dominant plant species at climax. A forest series is named for the projected climax tree species—the grand fir series includes every plant association where grand fir is presumed to be the dominant tree species at climax (Pfister and Arno 1980). Series is the highest level of the fine-scale portion of the Blue Mountains potential vegetation hierarchy (fig. 2).

shrub land—Land areas of sufficient size to be delineated as a mapping unit where the predominant vegetation life form consists of shrubs.

steppe—Open herbaceous vegetation, less than 1 meter high, with the tufts or plants discrete, yet sufficiently close together to dominate the landscape (Bailey 1998).

structure class (stage)—A stage or recognizable condition relating to the physical orientation and arrangement of vegetation; the size and arrangement (both vertical and horizontal) of trees and tree parts (O'Hara et al. 1996, Oliver and Larson 1996).

successional stage—A stage or recognizable condition of a plant community occurring during its development from bare ground to climax; coniferous forests in the Blue Mountains progress through six recognized stages: grass-forb, shrub-seedling, pole-sapling, young, mature, and old growth (Thomas 1979).

taxonomic unit—The basic set of classes or types making up a classification; in this document, potential vegetation taxonomic units are presented in figure 2.

union—A group of plant species used to represent a particular ecological environ-ment or microclimatic condition; a union typically consists of species that are similar in life form, phenology, or stature (Sampson 1939). The union includes a fraction of the total floristic composition for a vegetation type—only the combina-tion of species that is useful for vegetation classification purposes is designated as a union (Daubenmire 1968).

upland—Land that generally has a higher elevation than an adjacent alluvial plain, stream terrace, or riparian zone; or land above the foothill zone for a mountainous continuum (Dunster and Dunster 1996).

zonal—Areas of soil and vegetation largely controlled by the prevailing regional climate. Here climate, not exceptional landforms or rock types, determines the nature of soils and its associated vegetation (Kruckeberg 2002).

Species List

This list provides codes (symbols) and scientific names for plants mentioned in the text or in tables and figures. The Pacific Northwest Region (R6) codes and scientific names provided in the first two columns were taken from published pot-ential vegetation classifications for the Blue Mountains section (e.g., Crowe and Clausnitzer 1997, Johnson 2004, Johnson and Clausnitzer 1992, Johnson and Simon 1987, Johnson and Swanson 2005, Wells 2006).

Nomenclature for scientific plant names was revised when the U.S. Depart-ment of Agriculture adopted a national taxonomy called the PLANTS database. The third column provides the PLANTS database code for each of the plant species (USDA NRCS 2004). For plants whose nomenclature recently changed in the PLANTS database, the suggested synonym and synonym code is also provided as the fourth and fifth columns in the species list.

R6 code	Scientific name	PLANTS code	PLANTS synonym	Synonym code
ABGR	*Abies grandis* (Dougl.) Lindl.	ABGR		
ABLA2	*Abies lasiocarpa* (Hook.) Nutt.	ABLA		
ACGL	*Acer glabrum* Torr.	ACGL		
ADPE	*Adiantum pedatum* L.	ADPE		
AGCA	*Agropyron caninum* (L.) Beauv.	AGCA2	*Elymus caninus* (L.) L.	ELCA11
AGDI	*Agrostis diegoensis* Vasey	AGDI	*Agrostis pallens* Trin.	AGPA8
AGGL	*Agoseris glauca* (Pursh) Raf.	AGGL		
AGSP	*Agropyron spicatum* (Pursh) Scrib. & Smith	AGSP	*Pseudoroegneria spicata spicata* (Pursh) A. Löve	PSSPS
AGUR	*Agastache urticifolia* Kuntze	AGUR		
ALIN	*Alnus incana* (L.) Moench	ALIN2		
ALPR	*Alopecurus pratensis* L.	ALPR3		
ALRH	*Alnus rhombifolia* Nutt.	ALRH2		
ALRU	*Alnus rubra* Bong.	ALRU2		
ALSI	*Alnus sinuata* (Regel) Rydb.	ALSI3	*Alnus viridis sinuata* (Regel) A. & D. Löve	ALVIS
ALVA	*Allium validum* Wats.	ALVA		
AMAL	*Amelanchier alnifolia* Nutt.	AMAL2		
APAN	*Apocynum androsaemifolium* L.	APAN2		
ARAC2	*Arenaria aculeata* Wats.	ARAC2		
ARAR	*Artemisia arbuscula* Nutt.	ARAR8		
ARCA	*Artemisia cana* Pursh	ARCA13		
ARCO	*Arnica cordifolia* Hook.	ARCO9		
ARLO3	*Aristida longiseta* Stevc.	ARLO3	*Aristida purpurea longiseta* (Steud.) Vasey	ARPUL
ARLO	*Arnica longifolia* D.C. Eat.	ARLO6		
ARLU	*Artemisia ludoviciana* Nutt.	ARLU		
ARNE	*Arctostaphylos nevadensis* Gray	ARNE		
ARRI	*Artemisia rigida* (Nutt.) Gray	ARRI2		
ARTR2	*Artemisia tripartita* Rydb.	ARTR4		
ARTRV	*Artemisia tridentata vaseyana* (Rydb.) Beetle	ARTRV		
ASCA3	*Asarum caudatum* Lindl.	ASCA2		
ASCU4	*Astragalus cusickii cusickii* Gray	ASCUC2		
ASRE	*Astragalus reventus* Gray	ASRE5		
ATFI	*Athyrium filix-femina* (L.) Roth.	ATFI		
BASA	*Balsamorhiza sagittata* (Pursh) Nutt.	BASA3		
BEGL	*Betula glandulosa* Michx.	BEGL		
BEOC	*Betula occidentalis* Hook.	BEOC2		
BERE	*Berberis repens* Lindl.	BERE	*Mahonia repens* (Lindl.) G. Don	MARE11
BRCA	*Bromus carinatus* H. & A.	BRCA5		

R6 code	Scientific name	PLANTS code	PLANTS synonym	Synonym code
BROMU	*Bromus* L.	BROMU		
BRVU	*Bromus vulgaris* (Hook.) Shear	BRVU		
CAAM	*Carex amplifolia* Boott	CAAM10		
CAAQ	*Carex aquatilis* Wahl.	CAAQ		
CACA4	*Carex canescens* L.	CACA11		
CACA	*Calamagrostis canadensis* (Michx.) Beauv.	CACA4		
CACU	*Camassia cusickii* Wats.	CACU2		
CACU2	*Carex cusickii* Mack.	CACU5		
CADE	*Carex deweyana* Schw.	CADE9		
CADI	*Carex disperma* Dewey	CADI6		
CAEU	*Carex eurycarpa* Holm.	CAEU2	*Carex angustata* Boott	CAAN15
CAGE	*Carex geyeri* Boott	CAGE2		
CAHO	*Carex hoodii* Boott	CAHO5		
CAJO	*Carex jonesii* L. H. Bailey	CAJO		
CALA4	*Carex lasiocarpa* Ehrh.	CALA11		
CALA	*Carex laeviculmis* Meinsh.	CALA13		
CALA3	*Carex lanuginosa* Michx.	CALA30	*Carex pellita* Muhl. ex Willd.	CAPE42
CALE5	*Carex lenticularis* Michx.	CALE8		
CALE3	*Carex leporinella* Mack.	CALE9		
CALEL2	*Carex lenticularis lenticularis* Michx.	CALEL		
CALI	*Carex limosa* L.	CALI7		
CALU	*Carex luzulina* Olney	CALU7		
CAMI	*Carex microptera* Mack.	CAMI7		
CAMU2	*Carex muricata* L.	CAMU7		
CANE	*Carex nebrascensis* Dewey	CANE2		
CANI2	*Carex nigricans* C.A. Mey.	CANI2		
CANU4	*Carex nudata* Boott	CANU5		
CAPE	*Carex petasata* Dewey	CAPE7		
CAPR5	*Carex praegracilis* Boott	CAPR5		
CAREX	*Carex* L.	CAREX		
CARO	*Carex rossii* Boott	CARO5		
CARU	*Calamagrostis rubescens* Buckl.	CARU		
CASC3	*Carex scirpoidea* Michx.	CASC10		
CASC5	*Carex scopulorum* Holm	CASC12		
CASH	*Carex sheldonii* Mackenzie	CASH		
CASI2	*Carex simulata* Mack.	CASI2		
CAST	*Carex stipata* Muhl.	CAST5		
CASU4	*Carex subfusca* Boott	CASU6		

R6 code	Scientific name	PLANTS code	PLANTS synonym	Synonym code
CAUT	*Carex utriculata* Boott	CAUT		
CAVE	*Carex vesicaria* L.	CAVE6		
CELE	*Cercocarpus ledifolius* Nutt.	CELE3		
CERE2	*Celtis reticulata* Torr.	CERE2	*Celtis laevigata reticulata* (Torr.) L. Benson	CELAR
CEVE	*Ceanothus velutinus* Dougl. ex Hook.	CEVE		
CHNO	*Chamaecyparis nootkatensis* (D.Don) Spach	CHNO	*Cupressus nootkatensis* D. Don	CUNO
CHUM	*Chimaphila umbellata* (L.) Bart.	CHUM		
CILA2	*Cinna latifolia* (Trevir.) Griseb.	CILA2		
CLUN	*Clintonia uniflora* (Schult.) Kunth	CLUN2		
COOC2	*Coptis occidentalis* (Nutt.) T. & G.	COOC		
COST	*Cornus stolonifera* Michx.	COST4	*Cornus sericea sericea* L.	COSES
CRDO	*Crataegus douglasii* Lindl.	CRDO2		
CYTEF	*Cymopterus terebinthinus foeniculaceus* (T. & G.) Cronq.	CYTEF	*Pteryxia terebinthina foeniculacea* (Nutt. ex T. & G.) Mathias	PTTEF
DAIN	*Danthonia intermedia* Vasey	DAIN		
DAUN	*Danthonia unispicata* (Thurb.) Munro ex Macoun	DAUN		
DECE	*Deschampsia cespitosa* (L.) Beauv.	DECE	*Deschampsia caespitosa* (L.) Beauv.	DECA18
ELBE	*Eleocharis bella* (Piper) Svenson	ELBE		
ELCI	*Elymus cinereus* Scribn. & Smith	ELCI2	*Leymus cinereus* (Scribn. & Merr.) A. Löve	LECI4
ELGL	*Elymus glaucus* Buckl.	ELGL		
ELPA	*Eleocharis palustris* (L.) R. & S.	ELPA3		
ELPA2	*Eleocharis pauciflora* (Lightf.) Link	ELPA6	*Eleocharis quinqueflora* (F.X. Hartmann) Schwarz	ELQU2
EQAR	*Equisetum arvense* L.	EQAR		
ERDO	*Eriogonum douglasii* Benth.	ERDO		
ERFL	*Eriogonum flavum* Nutt.	ERFL4		
ERHE	*Eriogonum heracleoides* Nutt.	ERHE2		
ERIOG	*Eriogonum* L.	ERIOG		
ERPU	*Erigeron pumilus* Nutt.	ERPU2		
ERST2	*Eriogonum strictum* Benth.	ERST4		
ERUM	*Eriogonum umbellatum* Torr.	ERUM		
FEID	*Festuca idahoensis* Elmer	FEID		
FESC	*Festuca scabrella* Torr. ex Hook. [var. *major* Vasey]	FESCM	*Festuca campestris* Rydb.	FECA4
FEVI	*Festuca viridula* Vasey	FEVI		
FRALC	*Frasera albicaulis cusickii* C.L. Hitchc.	FRALC2		
GETR	*Geum triflorum* Pursh	GETR		
GLEL	*Glyceria elata* (Nash ex Rydb.) M.E. Jones	GLEL	*Glyceria striata* (Lam.) A.S. Hitchc.	GLST
GLNE	*Glossopetalon nevadense* Gray	GLNE	*Glossopetalon spinescens aridum* M.E. Jones	GLSPA
GYDR	*Gymnocarpium dryopteris* (L.) Newm.	GYDR		

R6 code	Scientific name	PLANTS code	PLANTS synonym	Synonym code
HELA	*Heracleum lanatum* Michx.	HELA4	*Heracleum maximum* Bartr.	HEMA80
HODI	*Holodiscus discolor* (Pursh) Maxim.	HODI		
IVGO	*Ivesia gordonii* (Hook.) T. & G.	IVGO		
JUBA	*Juncus balticus* Willd.	JUBA	*Juncus arcticus littoralis* (Engelm.) Hultén	JUARL
JUCO4	*Juncus communis* L.	JUCO6		
JUDR	*Juncus drummondii* E. Mey.	JUDR		
JUOC	*Juniperus occidentalis* Hook.	JUOC		
JUPA	*Juncus parryi* Engelm.	JUPA		
JUSC	*Juniperus scopulorum* Sarg.	JUSC2		
JUTE	*Juncus tenuis* Willd.	JUTE		
KAMI	*Kalmia microphylla* (Hook.) Heller	KAMI		
KOCR	*Koeleria cristata* Pers.	KOCR	*Koeleria macrantha* (Ledeb.) J.A. Schultes	KOMA
LECOW	*Lewisia columbiana wallowensis* C.L. Hitchc.	LECOW2	*Lewisia columbiana wallowensis* C.L. Hitchc.	LECOW
LEGL	*Ledum glandulosum* Nutt.	LEGL		
LEPY	*Lewisia pygmaea* (Gray) Robins.	LEPY2		
LIBO2	*Linnaea borealis* L.	LIBO3		
LICA2	*Ligusticum canbyi* Coult. & Rose	LICA2		
LINU	*Linanthastrum nuttallii* (Gray) Ewan	LINU4	*Leptosiphon nuttallii nuttallii* (Gray) J.M. Porter & L.A. Johnson	LENUN
LOIN	*Lonicera involucrata* (Rich.) Banks ex Spreng.	LOIN5		
LOLE	*Lomatium leptocarpum* (T. & G.) Coult. & Rose	LOLE2	*Lomatium bicolor leptocarpum* (Torr. & Gray) Schlessman	LOBIL
LUAR3	*Lupinus argenteus* Pursh	LUAR3		
LUHI	*Luzula hitchcockii* Hämet-Ahti	LUHI4	*Luzula glabrata hitchcockii* (Hämet-Ahti) Dorn	LUGLH
LULA2	*Lupinus laxiflorus* Dougl. ex Lindl.	LULA3	*Lupinus argenteus laxiflorus* (Dougl. ex Lindl.) Dorn	LUARL5
LUPIN	*Lupinus* L.	LUPIN		
LUSE	*Lupinus sericeus* Pursh	LUSE4		
MAGL	*Madia glomerata* Hook.	MAGL2		
MEBU	*Melica bulbosa* Geyer ex Porter & Coult.	MEBU		
MEFE	*Menziesia ferruginea* Smith	MEFE		
METR	*Menyanthes trifoliata* L.	METR3		
MILE	*Mimulus lewisii* Pursh	MILE2		
MOOD	*Monardella odoratissima* Benth.	MOOD		
NUPO	*Nuphar polysepala* Engelm.	NUPO2	*Nuphar lutea polysepala* (Engelm.) E.O. Beal	NULUP
OPPO	*Opuntia polyacantha* Haw.	OPPO		
OREX	*Oryzopsis exigua* Thurb.	OREX	*Piptatherum exiguum* (Thurb.) Dorn	PIEX3
PECO	*Pedicularis contorta* Benth.	PECO		

R6 code	Scientific name	PLANTS code	PLANTS synonym	Synonym code
PEFRP	Petasites frigidus palmatus (Ait.) Cronq.	PEFRP		
PEGA	Penstemon gairdneri Hook.	PEGA		
PENST	Penstemon Schmidel	PENST		
PERA3	Peraphyllum ramosissimum Nutt.	PERA4		
PESP2	Penstemon spatulatus Pennell	PESP2		
PHAR	Phalaris arundinacea L.	PHAR3		
PHAU	Phlox austromontana Cov.	PHAU3		
PHCA3	Physocarpus capitatus (Pursh) Kuntze	PHCA11		
PHCO2	Phlox colubrina Wherry & Constance	PHCO10		
PHEM	Phyllodoce empetriformis (Sm.) D. Don	PHEM		
PHLE2	Philadelphus lewisii Pursh	PHLE4		
PHLOX	Phlox L.	PHLOX		
PHMA	Physocarpus malvaceus (Greene) Kuntze	PHMA5		
PHOR	Physaria oregona S. Wats.	PHOR2		
PIAL	Pinus albicaulis Engelm.	PIAL		
PICO	Pinus contorta Dougl. ex Loud.	PICO		
PIEN	Picea engelmannii Parry ex Engelm.	PIEN		
PIFL	Pinus flexilis James	PIFL2		
PIMO	Pinus monticola Dougl. ex D. Don	PIMO3		
PIPO	Pinus ponderosa Dougl. ex Loud.	PIPO		
POBU	Poa bulbosa L.	POBU		
POCU	Poa cusickii Vasey	POCU3		
POFR	Potentilla fruticosa L.	POFR4	Dasiphora fruticosa floribunda (Pursh) Kartesz	DAFRF
POGL	Potentilla glandulosa Lindl.	POGL9		
POMU	Polystichum munitum (Kaulf.) Presl.	POMU		
PONEW	Poa nervosa wheeleri (Vasey) C.L. Hitchc.	PONEW	Poa wheeleri Vasey	POWH2
POPH	Polygonum phytolaccifolium Meisn. ex Small	POPH		
POPR	Poa pratensis L.	POPR		
POPU	Polemonium pulcherrimum Hook.	POPU3		
POSA3	Poa sandbergii Vasey	POSA12	Poa secunda J. Presl	POSE
POTR2	Populus trichocarpa T. & G. ex Hook.	POTR15	Populus balsamifera trichocarpa (T. & G. ex Hook.) Brayshaw	POBAT
POTR	Populus tremuloides Michx.	POTR5		
PREM	Prunus emarginata (Dougl.) Walpers	PREM		
PSME	Pseudotsuga menziesii (Mirbel) Franco	PSME		
PTAQ	Pteridium aquilinum (L.) Kuhn	PTAQ		
PUPA	Puccinellia pauciflora (J. Presl.) Munz	PUPA3	Torreyochloa pallida pauciflora (J. Presl) J.I. Davis	TOPAP3
PUTR	Purshia tridentata (Pursh) DC.	PUTR2		

R6 code	Scientific name	PLANTS code	PLANTS synonym	Synonym code
RHAL2	Rhamnus alnifolia L'Hér	RHAL		
RHAL	Rhododendron albiflorum Hook.	RHAL2		
RHGL	Rhus glabra L.	RHGL		
RIBES	Ribes L.	RIBES		
RIMO	Ribes montigenum McClatchie	RIMO2		
ROSA	Rosa L.	ROSA5		
RUBA	Rubus bartonianus Peck	RUBA		
RUBUS	Rubus L.	RUBUS		
RUDI	Rubus discolor Weihe & Nees	RUDI2	Rubus armeniacus Focke	RUAR9
RUOC	Rudbeckia occidentalis Nutt.	RUOC2		
RUPA	Rubus parviflorus Nutt.	RUPA		
SAAR4	Saxifraga arguta D. Don	SAAR13	Saxifraga odontoloma Piper	SAOD2
SAAR5	Salix arctica Pall.	SAAR27		
SABO2	Salix boothii Dorn	SABO2		
SACO2	Salix commutata Bebb.	SACO2		
SADR	Salix drummondiana Barratt	SADR		
SAEA	Salix eastwoodiae Cockerell ex Heller	SAEA		
SAEX	Salix exigua Nutt.	SAEX		
SAFA	Salix farriae Ball	SAFA		
SALA2	Salix lasiandra Benth.	SALA5	Salix lucida lasiandra (Benth.) E. Murr.	SALUL
SALE	Salix lemmonii Bebb.	SALE		
SALIX	Salix L.	SALIX		
SARI	Salix rigida Muhl. [mackenzieana (Hook.) Cronq.]	SARIM4	Salix prolixa Anderss.	SAPR3
SASC	Salix scouleriana Barratt	SASC		
SASI2	Salix sitchensis Sanson	SASI2		
SATW	Salix tweedyi (Bebb.) Ball	SATW		
SCAN	Scutellaria angustifolia Pursh	SCAN3		
SCMI	Scirpus microcarpus Presl.	SCMI2		
SELA2	Sedum lanceolatum Torr.	SELA		
SETR	Senecio triangularis Hook.	SETR		
SIHY	Sitanion hystrix (Nutt.) J.G. Sm.	SIHY	Elymus elymoides elymoides (Raf.) Swezey	ELELE
SPAN	Sparganium angustifolium Michx.	SPAN2		
SPBE	Spiraea betulifolia Pall.	SPBE2		
SPCR	Sporobolus cryptandrus (Torr.) Gray	SPCR		

R6 code	Scientific name	PLANTS code	PLANTS synonym	Synonym code
STAM	Streptopus amplexifolius (L.) DC.	STAM2		
STLE2	Stipa lemmonii (Vasey) Scribn.	STLE2	Achnatherum lemmonii lemmonii (Vasey) Barkworth	ACLEL
STOC	Stipa occidentalis Thurb. ex Wats.	STOC2	Achnatherum occidentale occidentale (Thurb.) Barkworth	ACOCO
SYAL	Symphoricarpos albus (L.) Blake	SYAL		
SYOR	Symphoricarpos oreophilus Gray	SYOR2		
TABR	Taxus brevifolia Nutt.	TABR2		
TRCA3	Trautvetteria caroliniensis (Walt.) Vail	TRCA		
TRMA	Trifolium macrocephalum (Pursh) Poir.	TRMA3		
TSME	Tsuga mertensiana (Bong.) Carr.	TSME		
TYLA	Typha latifolia L.	TYLA		
VAME	Vaccinium membranaceum Dougl. ex Hook.	VAME		
VASC	Vaccinium scoparium Leib.	VASC		
VAUL	Vaccinium uliginosum L.	VAUL		
VEAM	Veronica americana Schwein. ex Benth.	VEAM2		
VERAT	Veratrum L.	VERAT		
XETE	Xerophyllum tenax (Pursh) Nutt.	XETE		

Acknowledgments

The authors acknowledge the following individuals for their contributions to the development of information presented in this report (note that national forest affiliation and work location information was accurate when the potential vegetation work described in this report was completed).

Charlene Bucha-Gentry, Umatilla National Forest, Heppner, OR

Katie Countryman, Wallowa-Whitman National Forest, Baker City, OR

Steve Fletcher, Wallowa-Whitman National Forest, Baker City, OR

Bill Gamble, Malheur National Forest, John Day, OR

Les Holsapple, Umatilla National Forest, Pendleton, OR

Lyle Jensen, Umatilla National Forest, Pendleton, OR

Don Justice, Umatilla National Forest, Pendleton, OR

John Keersemaker, Umatilla National Forest, Pendleton, OR

Bill McArthur, Malheur National Forest, John Day, OR

Chuck Quimby, Wallowa-Whitman National Forest, Baker City, OR

Scott Riley, Umatilla National Forest, Pendleton, OR

Victoria Rockwell, Wallowa-Whitman National Forest, Baker City, OR

Ray Smith, Malheur National Forest, John Day, OR

Ed Uebler, Malheur National Forest, John Day, OR

Karl Urban, Umatilla National Forest, Pendleton, OR

Gene Yates, Malheur National Forest, John Day, OR

This report benefited greatly from technical peer review by Craig Busskohl (soil scientist, Umatilla National Forest), Tom DeMeo (plant ecologist, Pacific Northwest Regional Office), Becky Gravenmier (planning specialist, Pacific Northwest Research Station), Paul Oester (extension forester for Union County, Oregon State University), Ayn Shlisky (plant ecologist, The Nature Conservancy) and Mike Simpson (plant ecologist, Central Oregon Area Ecology Program).

References

Agee, J.K. 1993. Fire ecology of Pacific Northwest forests. Washington, DC: Island Press. 493 p.

Agee, J.K. 1998. The landscape ecology of western forest fire regimes. Northwest Science. 72(special issue): 24–34.

Alexander, R.R. 1985. Major habitat types, community types, and plant communities in the Rocky Mountains. Gen. Tech. Rep. RM-123. Fort Collins, CO: U.S. Department of Agriculture, Forest Service, Rocky Mountain Forest and Range Experiment Station. 105 p.

Allaby, M., ed. 1998. The concise Oxford dictionary of ecology. 2nd ed. New York: Oxford University Press. 440 p.

Bailey, R.G. 1995. Description of the ecoregions of the United States. Misc. Publ. 1391. Washington, DC: U.S. Department of Agriculture, Forest Service. 108 p.

Bailey, R.G. 1996. Ecosystem geography. New York: Springer-Verlag. 204 p.

Bailey, R.G. 1998. Ecoregions map of North America: explanatory note. Misc. Publ. 1548. Washington, DC: U.S. Department of Agriculture, Forest Service. 10 p.

Bergeron, Y.; Bouchard, A. 1984. Use of ecological groups in analysis and classification of plant communities in a section of western Quebec. Vegetatio. 56: 45–63.

Beukema, S.J.; Kurz, W.A.; Pinkham, C.B.; Milosheva, K.; Frid, L. 2003. Vegetation dynamics development tool, user's guide, version 4.4. Vancouver, BC: Essa Technologies Ltd. 234 p.

Blackwood, J.D. 1998 (December 11). Historical percentages for use with HRV analyses; file designation 2430/2600 memorandum to District Rangers. Pendleton, OR: U.S. Department of Agriculture, Forest Service, Umatilla National Forest, Supervisor's Office. 8 p. On file with: USDA Forest Service, Umatilla National Forest, 2517 SW Hailey Avenue, Pendleton, OR 97801.

Blumer, J.C. 1911. Change of aspect with altitude. Plant World. 14: 236–248.

Botanical Resources Group. 2004. A pocket checklist of plants of the Umatilla National Forest, Oregon and Washington. 7th ed. FS-SO-06-04. Pendleton, OR: U.S. Department of Agriculture, Forest Service, Umatilla National Forest. 152 p.

Botkin, D.B. 1990. Discordant harmonies: a new ecology for the twenty-first century. New York: Oxford University Press. 241 p.

Brohman, R.; Bryant, L., eds. 2005. Existing vegetation classification and mapping technical guide. Gen. Tech. Rep. WO-67. Washington, DC: U.S. Department of Agriculture, Forest Service, Ecosystem Management Coordination Staff. 305 p.

Brown, R.T.; Agee, J.K.; Franklin, J.F. 2004. Forest restoration and fire: principles in the context of place. Conservation Biology. 18(4): 903–912.

Bryce, S.A.; Omernik, J.M. 1997. Section 2–level IV ecoregions of the Blue Mountains ecoregion of Oregon, Washington, and Idaho. In: Clarke, S.E.; Bryce, S.A., eds. Hierarchical subdivisions of the Columbia Plateau and Blue Mountains ecoregions, Oregon and Washington. Gen. Tech. Rep. PNW-GTR-395. Portland, OR: U.S. Department of Agriculture, Forest Service, Pacific Northwest Research Station: 24–55.

Clarke, S.E.; Bryce, S.A., eds. 1997. Hierarchical subdivisions of the Columbia Plateau and Blue Mountains ecoregions, Oregon and Washington. Gen. Tech. Rep. PNW-GTR-395. Portland, OR: U.S. Department of Agriculture, Forest Service, Pacific Northwest Research Station. 114 p.

Clausnitzer, R.R. 1993. The grand fir series of northeastern Oregon and southeastern Washington: successional stages and management guide. Tech. Publ. R6-ECO-TP-050-93. [Place of publication unknown]: U.S. Department of Agriculture, Forest Service, Pacific Northwest Region, Wallowa-Whitman National Forest. 193 p.

Cleland, D.T.; Avers, P.E.; McNab, W.H.; Jensen, M.E.; Bailey, R.G.; King, T.; Russell, W.E. 1997. National hierarchical framework of ecological units. In: Boyce, M.S.; Haney, A., eds. Ecosystem management: applications for sustainable forest and wildlife resources. New Haven, CT: Yale University Press: 181-200.

Cochran, P.H.; Geist, J.M.; Clemens, D.L.; Clausnitzer, R.R.; Powell, D.C. 1994. Suggested stocking levels for forest stands in northeastern Oregon and southeastern Washington. Res. Note PNW-RN-513. Portland, OR: U.S. Department of Agriculture, Forest Service, Pacific Northwest Research Station. 21 p.

Comer, P.; Faber-Langendoen, D.; Evans, R.; Gawler, S.; Josse, C.; Kittel, G.; Menard, S.; Pyne, M.; Reid, M.; Schulz, K.; Snow, K.; Teague, J. 2003. Ecological systems of the United States: a working classification of U.S. terrestrial ecosystems. Arlington, VA: NatureServe. 75 p.

Cook, J.E. 1996. Implications of modern successional theory for habitat typing: a review. Forest Science. 42(1): 67–75.

Crane, M.F.; Fischer, W.C. 1986. Fire ecology of the forest habitat types of central Idaho. Gen. Tech. Rep. INT-218. Ogden, UT: U.S. Department of Agriculture, Forest Service, Intermountain Research Station. 86 p.

Crowe, E.A.; Clausnitzer, R.R. 1997. Mid-montane wetland plant associations of the Malheur, Umatilla and Wallowa-Whitman National Forests. Tech. Pap. R6-NR-ECOL-TP-22-97. Baker City, OR: U.S. Department of Agriculture, Forest Service, Pacific Northwest Region, Wallowa-Whitman National Forest. 299 p.

Daubenmire, R. 1952. Forest vegetation of northern Idaho and adjacent Washington, and its bearing on concepts of vegetation classification. Ecological Monographs. 22(4): 301–330.

Daubenmire, R. 1961. Vegetative indicators of rate of height growth in ponderosa pine. Forest Science. 7(1): 24–34.

Daubenmire, R. 1966. Vegetation: identification of typal communities. Science. 151: 291–298.

Daubenmire, R. 1968. Plant communities, a textbook of plant synecology. New York: Harper and Row. 300 p.

Daubenmire, R. 1973. A comparison of approaches to the mapping of forest land for intensive management. Forestry Chronicle. 49(2): 87–91.

Daubenmire, R. 1976. The use of vegetation in assessing the productivity of forest lands. Botanical Review. 42(2): 115–143.

Davis, L.S.; Johnson, K.N.; Bettinger, P.S.; Howard, T.E. 2001. Forest management: to sustain ecological, economic, and social values. 4th ed. New York: McGraw-Hill. 804 p.

Deitschmann, G.H. 1973. Mapping of habitat types throughout a national forest. Gen. Tech. Rep. INT-11. Ogden, UT: U.S. Department of Agriculture, Forest Service, Intermountain Forest and Range Experiment Station. 14 p.

Despain, D.G.; Weaver, T.; Aspinall, R.J. 2001. A rule-based model for mapping potential exotic plant distribution. Western North American Naturalist. 61(4): 428–433.

Dunster, J.; Dunster, K. 1996. Dictionary of natural resource management. Vancouver, BC: UBC Press. 363 p.

Emmingham, W.H.; Oester, P.T.; Fitzgerald, S.A.; Filip, G.M.; Edge, W.D. 2005. Ecology and management of eastern Oregon forests: a comprehensive manual for forest managers. Manual 12. Corvallis, OR: Oregon State University, Extension Service. 208 p.

Everett, R.L.; Lehmkuhl, J.F. 1999. Restoring biodiversity on public forest lands through disturbance and patch management irrespective of land-use allocation. In: Baydack, R.K.; Campa, H.; Haufler, J.B., eds. Practical approaches to the conservation of biological diversity. Washington, DC: Island Press: 87–105.

Eyre, F.H. 1980. Forest cover types of the United States and Canada. Washington, DC: Society of American Foresters. 148 p.

Flint, H.R. 1925. Fire resistance of northern Rocky Mountain conifers. Idaho Forester. 7: 7–10, 41–43.

Franklin, J.F.; Agee, J.K. 2003. Forging a science-based national forest fire policy. Issues in Science and Technology. 20(1): 59–66.

Garrison, G.A.; Skovlin, J.M.; Poulton, C.E.; Winward, A.H. 1976. Northwest range plant names and symbols for ecosystem inventory and analysis. 4th ed. Gen. Tech. Rep. PNW-46. Portland, OR: U.S. Department of Agriculture, Forest Service, Pacific Northwest Forest and Range Experiment Station. 263 p.

Graham, R.T.; McCaffrey, S.; Jain, T.B., tech. eds. 2004. Science basis for changing forest structure to modify wildfire behavior and severity. Gen. Tech. Rep. RMRS-GTR-120. Fort Collins, CO: U.S. Department of Agriculture, Forest Service, Rocky Mountain Experiment Station. 43 p.

Habeck, J.R.; Mutch, R.W. 1973. Fire-dependent forests in the northern Rocky Mountains. Quaternary Research. 3: 408–424.

Hall, F.C. 1989. Plant community classification: from concept to application. In: Ferguson, D.E.; Morgan, P.; Johnson, F.D., comps. Proceedings—land classifications based on vegetation: applications for resource management. Gen. Tech. Rep. INT-257. Ogden, UT: U.S. Department of Agriculture, Forest Service, Intermountain Research Station: 41–48.

Hall, F.C. 1998. Pacific Northwest ecoclass codes for seral and potential natural communities. Gen. Tech. Rep. PNW-GTR-418. Portland, OR: U.S. Department of Agriculture, Forest Service, Pacific Northwest Research Station. 290 p.

Hall, F.C.; Bryant, L.; Clausnitzer, R.; Geier-Hayes, K.; Keane, R.; Kertis, J.; Shlisky, A.; Steele, R. 1995. Definitions and codes for seral status and structure of vegetation. Gen. Tech. Rep. PNW-GTR-363. Portland, OR: U.S. Department of Agriculture, Forest Service, Pacific Northwest Research Station. 39 p.

Hann, W.; Havlina, D.; Shlisky, A. 2005. Interagency fire regime condition class guidebook, version 1.2. http://www.frcc.gov. (January 2006).

Hann, W.J.; Jones, J.L.; Karl, M.G.; Hessburg, P.F.; Keane, R.E.; Long, D.G.; Menakis, J.P.; McNicoll, C.H.; Leonard, S.G.; Gravenmier, R.A.; Smith, B.G. 1997. Chapter 3: landscape dynamics of the basin. In: Quigley, T.M.; Arbelbide, S.J., tech. eds. An assessment of ecosystem components in the interior Columbia basin and portions of the Klamath and Great Basins: volume 2. Gen. Tech. Rep. PNW-GTR-405. Portland, OR: U.S. Department of Agriculture, Forest Service, Pacific Northwest Research Station: 337–1055.

Hanson, E. 2000. PLANTS; alphabetical list, current and old names. Portland, OR: U.S. Department of Agriculture, Forest Service, Portland Forestry Sciences Laboratory, Forest Inventory and Analysis. 436 p.

Haynes, R.W.; Graham, R.T.; Quigley, T.M. 1996. A framework for ecosystem management in the interior Columbia basin and portions of the Klamath and Great Basins. Gen. Tech. Rep. PNW-GTR-374. Portland, OR: U.S. Department of Agriculture, Forest Service, Pacific Northwest Research Station. 68 p.

Helms, J.A., ed. 1998. The dictionary of forestry. Bethesda, MD: Society of American Foresters. 210 p.

Huff, M.H.; Ottmar, R.D.; Alvarado, E.; Everett, R.L.; Vihnanek, R.E.; Lehmkuhl, J.F.; Hessburg, P.F. 1995. Historical and current forest landscapes in eastern Oregon and Washington. Part II: Linking vegetation characteristics to potential fire behavior and related smoke production. Gen. Tech. Rep. PNW-GTR-355. Portland, OR: U.S. Department of Agriculture, Forest Service, Pacific Northwest Research Station. 43 p.

Huston, M.; Smith, T. 1987. Plant succession: life history and competition. American Naturalist. 130(2): 168–198.

Jensen, M.; Goodman, I.; Brewer, K.; Frost, T.; Ford, G.; Nesser, J. 1997. Chapter 2: biophysical environments of the basin. In: Quigley, T.M.; Arbelbide, S.J., tech. eds. An assessment of ecosystem components in the interior Columbia basin and portions of the Klamath and Great Basins: volume 1. Gen. Tech. Rep. PNW-GTR-405. Portland, OR: U.S. Department of Agriculture, Forest Service, Pacific Northwest Research Station: 99–320.

Johnson, C.G., Jr. 2004. Alpine and subalpine vegetation of the Wallowa, Seven Devils and Blue Mountains. Tech. Publ. R6-NR-ECOL-TP-03-04. Portland, OR: U.S. Department of Agriculture, Forest Service, Pacific Northwest Region. 612 p.

Johnson, C.G., Jr.; Clausnitzer, R.R. 1992. Plant associations of the Blue and Ochoco Mountains. Tech. Publ. R6-ERW-TP-036-92. Portland, OR: U.S. Department of Agriculture, Forest Service, Pacific Northwest Region, Wallowa-Whitman National Forest. 164 p.

Johnson, C.G., Jr.; Simon, S.A. 1987. Plant associations of the Wallowa-Snake province. Tech. Publ. R6-ECOL-TP-225b-86. Baker City, OR: U.S. Department of Agriculture, Forest Service, Pacific Northwest Region, Wallowa-Whitman National Forest. 272 p.

Johnson, C.G., Jr.; Swanson, D.K. 2005. Bunchgrass plant communities of the Blue and Ochoco Mountains: a guide for managers. Gen. Tech. Rep. PNW-GTR-641. Portland, OR: U.S. Department of Agriculture, Forest Service, Pacific Northwest Research Station. 119 p.

Johnson, K.N.; Swanson, F.; Herring, M.; Greene, S., eds. 1999. Bioregional assessments: science at the crossroads of management and policy. Washington, DC: Island Press. 398 p.

Kelly, A.; Powell, D.C.; Riggs, R.A. 2005. Predicting potential natural vegetation in an interior Northwest landscape using classification tree modeling and a GIS. Western Journal of Applied Forestry. 20(2): 117–127.

Kimmins, J.P. 1997. Forest ecology; a foundation for sustainable management. 2nd ed. Upper Saddle River, NJ: Prentice Hall. 596 p.

Klinka, K.; Carter R.E. 1980. Ecology and silviculture of the most productive ecosystems for growth of Douglas-fir in southwestern British Columbia. Land Management Rep. 6. Victoria, BC: British Columbia Ministry of Forests, Information Services Branch. 12 p.

Kruckeberg, A.R. 2002. Geology and plant life: the effects of landforms and rock types on plants. Seattle, WA: University of Washington Press. 362 p.

Küchler, A.W. 1964. Potential natural vegetation of the conterminous United States: manual to accompany the map. Spec. Publ. 36. New York: American Geographical Society. 156 p.

Kurz, W.A.; Beukema, S.J.; Klenner, W.; Greenough, J.A.; Robinson, D.C.E.; Sharpe, A.D.; Webb, T.M. 2000. TELSA: the tool for exploratory landscape scenario analyses. Computers and Electronics in Agriculture. 27: 227–242.

Levin, S.A. 1992. The problem of pattern and scale in ecology. Ecology. 73: 1943–1967.

Losensky, B.J. 1994. Historical vegetation types of the interior Columbia River basin. Prepared under contract INT-94951-RJVA. Portland, OR: U.S. Department of Agriculture, Forest Service, Pacific Northwest Research Station, Interior Columbia Basin Ecosystem Management Project. 108 p. http://www.icbemp.gov/science/losensky.pdf. (January 2006).

Manning, M.E.; Engelking, L.D. 1997. Report on the riparian plant association groups and associated valley bottom types of the Columbia River basin. Second review draft of unpublished report prepared for USDA Forest Service. Portland, OR: U.S. Department of Agriculture, Forest Service, Pacific Northwest Research Station, Interior Columbia Basin Ecosystem Management Project. 133 p. http://www.icbemp.gov/science/manning.pdf. (January 2006).

Maxwell, J.R.; Edwards, C.J.; Jensen, M.E.; Paustian, S.J.; Parrott, H.; Hill, D.M. 1995. A hierarchical framework of aquatic ecological units in North America (nearctic zone). Gen. Tech. Rep. NC-176. St. Paul, MN: U.S. Department of Agriculture, Forest Service, North Central Forest Experiment Station. 72 p.

McCook, L.J. 1994. Understanding ecological community succession: causal models and theories, a review. Vegetatio. 110: 115–147.

McCune, B.; Allen, T.F.H. 1985a. Forest dynamics in the Bitterroot Canyons, Montana. Canadian Journal of Botany. 63: 377–383.

McCune, B.; Allen, T.F.H. 1985b. Will similar forests develop on similar sites? Canadian Journal of Botany. 63: 367–376.

McDonald, G.I. 1991. Connecting forest productivity to behavior of soil-borne diseases. In: Harvey, A.E.; Neuenschwander, L.F., comps. Proceedings—management and productivity of western-montane forest soils. Gen. Tech. Rep. INT-280. Ogden, UT: U.S. Department of Agriculture, Forest Service, Intermountain Research Station: 129–144.

McNab, W.H.; Avers, P.E. 1994. Ecological subregions of the United States: section descriptions. WO-WSA-5. Washington, DC: U.S. Department of Agriculture, Forest Service, Ecosystem Management. [Irregular pagination].

Meurisse, R.T.; Robbie, W.A.; Niehoff, J.; Ford, G. 1991. Dominant soil formation processes and properties in western-montane forest types and landscapes—some implications for productivity and management. In: Harvey, A.E.; Neuenschwander, L.F., comps. Proceedings—management and productivity of western-montane forest soils. Gen. Tech. Rep. INT-280. Ogden, UT: U.S. Department of Agriculture, Forest Service, Intermountain Research Station: 7–19.

Morgan, P.; Bunting, S.C.; Black, A.E.; Merrill, T.; Barrett, S. 1996. Fire regimes in the interior Columbia River basin: past and present. Final report for contract RJVA-INT-94913: coarse-scale classification and mapping of disturbance regimes in the Columbia River basin. Portland, OR: U.S. Department of Agriculture, Forest Service, Pacific Northwest Research Station, Interior Columbia Basin Ecosystem Management Project. 37 p. http://www.icbemp.gov/science/morgan.pdf. (January 2006).

Noble, I.R.; Slatyer, R.O. 1980. The use of vital attributes to predict successional changes in plant communities subject to recurrent disturbances. Vegetatio. 43: 5–21.

O'Hara, K.L.; Latham, P.A.; Hessburg, P.; Smith, B.G. 1996. A structural classification for inland Northwest forest vegetation. Western Journal of Applied Forestry. 11(3): 97–102.

Oliver, C.D.; Larson, B.C. 1996. Forest stand dynamics. Update ed. New York: John Wiley & Sons. 520 p.

Patterson, P.A.; Neiman, K.E.; Tonn, J.R. 1985. Field guide to forest plants of northern Idaho. Gen. Tech. Rep. INT-180. Ogden, UT: U.S. Department of Agriculture, Forest Service, Intermountain Research Station. 246 p.

Peterson, D.L.; Johnson, M.C.; Agee, J.K.; Jain, T.B.; McKenzie, D.; Reinhardt, E.D. 2005. Forest structure and fire hazard in dry forests of the Western United States. Gen. Tech. Rep. PNW-GTR-628. Portland, OR: U.S. Department of Agriculture, Forest Service, Pacific Northwest Research Station. 30 p.

Pfister, R.D.; Arno, S.F. 1980. Classifying forest habitat types based on potential climax vegetation. Forest Science. 26(1): 52–70.

Powell, D.C., comp. 1998. Potential natural vegetation of the Umatilla National Forest. 31 p. Unpublished report. On file with: USDA Forest Service, Umatilla National Forest, 2517 SW Hailey Avenue, Pendleton, OR 97801.

Powell, D.C. 1999. Suggested stocking levels for forest stands in northeastern Oregon and southeastern Washington: an implementation guide for the Umatilla National Forest. Tech. Publ. F14-SO-TP-03-99. Pendleton, OR: U.S. Department of Agriculture, Forest Service, Pacific Northwest Region, Umatilla National Forest. 300 p.

Powell, D.C. 2000. Potential vegetation, disturbance, plant succession, and other aspects of forest ecology. Tech. Publ. F14-SO-TP-09-00. Pendleton, OR: U.S. Department of Agriculture, Forest Service, Pacific Northwest Region, Umatilla National Forest. 88 p.

Powell, D.C. 2005. Tree density thresholds related to crown fire susceptibility. 20 p. Unpublished report. On file with: USDA Forest Service, Umatilla National Forest, 2517 SW Hailey Avenue, Pendleton, OR 97801.

Quigley, T.M.; Arbelbide, S.J., tech. eds. 1997. An assessment of ecosystem components in the interior Columbia basin and portions of the Klamath and Great Basins. Gen. Tech. Rep. PNW-GTR-405. Portland, OR: U.S. Department of Agriculture, Forest Service, Pacific Northwest Research Station. 4 volumes.

Quigley, T.M.; Cole, H.B. 1997. Highlighted scientific findings of the Interior Columbia Basin Ecosystem Management Project. Gen. Tech. Rep. PNW-GTR-404. Portland, OR: U.S. Department of Agriculture, Forest Service, Pacific Northwest Research Station. 34 p.

Quigley, T.M.; Haynes, R.W.; Graham, R.T. 1996. Integrated scientific assessment for ecosystem management in the interior Columbia basin. Gen. Tech. Rep. PNW-GTR-382. Portland, OR: U.S. Department of Agriculture, Forest Service, Pacific Northwest Research Station. 303 p.

Reid, M.; Bourgeron, P.; Humphries, H.; Jensen, M., comps. and eds. 1995. Documentation of the modeling of potential vegetation at three spatial scales using biophysical settings in the Columbia River basin assessment area. 354 p. Unpublished final report for contract #53-04HI-6890. http://www.icbemp.gov/science/reid_1.pdf and http://www.icbemp.gov/science/reid_2.pdf. (January 2006).

Regional Ecosystem Office [REO]. 1995. Ecosystem analysis at the watershed scale: federal guide for watershed analysis. Version 2.2. Portland, OR: Regional Ecosystem Office. 26 p.

Roberts, D.W. 1996. Modelling forest dynamics with vital attributes and fuzzy systems theory. Ecological Modelling. 90: 161–173.

Rydberg, P.A. 1916. Vegetative life zones of the Rocky Mountain region. Memoirs of the New York Botanical Garden. 6: 477–499.

Sampson, A.W. 1939. Plant indicators–concept and status. Botanical Review. 5(3): 155–206.

Schmidt, K.M.; Menakis, J.P.; Hardy, C.C.; Hann, W.J.; Bunnell, D.L. 2002. Development of coarse-scale spatial data for wildland fire and fuel management. Gen. Tech. Rep. RMRS-GTR-87. Fort Collins, CO: U.S. Department of Agriculture, Forest Service, Rocky Mountain Research Station. 41 p. [and CD-ROM].

Schmitt, C.; Powell, D.C. 2005. Rating forest stands for insect and disease susceptibility: a simplified approach. Version 2.0. Publ. BMPMSC-05-01. La Grande, OR: U.S. Department of Agriculture, Forest Service, Pacific Northwest Region, Umatilla and Wallowa-Whitman National Forests. 20 p.

Seaber, P.R.; Kapinos, F.P.; Knapp, G.L. 1987. Hydrologic unit maps. Water Supply Paper 2294. Corvallis, OR: U.S. Geological Survey. 63 p.

Shiflet, T.N., ed. 1994. Rangeland cover types of the United States. Denver, CO: Society for Range Management. 152 p.

Smith, T.; Huston, M. 1989. A theory of the spatial and temporal dynamics of plant communities. Vegetatio. 83: 49–69.

Starker, T.J. 1934. Fire resistance in the forest. Journal of Forestry. 32(4): 462–467.

Stauffer, R.C. 1957. Haeckel, Darwin, and ecology. Quarterly Review of Biology. 32(2): 138–144.

Steele, R.; Pfister, R.D.; Ryker, R.A.; Kittams, J.A. 1981. Forest habitat types of central Idaho. Gen. Tech. Rep. INT-114. Ogden, UT: U.S. Department of Agriculture, Forest Service, Intermountain Forest and Range Experiment Station. 138 p.

Steele, R.; Williams, R.E.; Weatherby, J.C.; Reinhardt, E.D.; Hoffman, J.T.; Thier, R.W. 1996. Stand hazard rating for central Idaho forests. Gen. Tech. Rep. INT-GTR-332. Ogden, UT: U.S. Department of Agriculture, Forest Service, Intermountain Research Station. 29 p.

Swanson, F.J.; Kratz, T.K.; Caine, N.; Woodmansee, R.G. 1988. Landform effects on ecosystem patterns and processes. BioScience. 38(2): 92–98.

Tansley, A.G. 1935. The use and abuse of vegetational concepts and terms. Ecology. 16(3): 284–307.

Thomas, J.W., tech. ed. 1979. Wildlife habitats in managed forests: the Blue Mountains of Oregon and Washington. Agric. Handb. 553. Washington, DC: U.S. Department of Agriculture, Forest Service. 512 p.

U.S. Department of Agriculture, Forest Service. 1995. Revised interim direction establishing riparian, ecosystem and wildlife standards for timber sales; Regional Forester's Forest Plan Amendment #2. Portland, OR: Pacific Northwest Region. 14 p.

U.S. Department of Agriculture, Forest Service. 1996. Status of the interior Columbia basin: summary of scientific findings. Gen. Tech. Rep. PNW-GTR-385. Portland, OR: Pacific Northwest Research Station; U.S. Department of the Interior, Bureau of Land Management. 144 p.

U.S. Department of Agriculture, Forest Service. 2002. Establishment of a potential vegetation hierarchy for forest planning. 21 p. Unpublished report. On file with: USDA Forest Service, Umatilla National Forest, 2517 SW Hailey Avenue, Pendleton, OR 97801.

U.S. Department of Agriculture, Natural Resources Conservation Service [USDA NRCS]. 2003. Keys to soil taxonomy. 9th ed. Washington, DC: Soil Survey Staff. 332 p.

U.S. Department of Agriculture, Natural Resources Conservation Service [USDA NRCS]. 2004. The PLANTS database, version 3.5 [Database]. Baton Rouge, LA: National Plant Data Center. http://plants.usda.gov. (December 2006).

Weaver, T.; Gustafson, D.; Lichthardt, J. 2001. Exotic plants in early and late seral vegetation of fifteen northern Rocky Mountain environments (HTs). Western North American Naturalist. 61(4): 417–427.

Wells, A.F. 2006. Deep canyon and subalpine riparian and wetland plant associations of the Malheur, Umatilla, and Wallowa-Whitman National Forests. Gen. Tech. Rep. GTR-PNW-682. Portland, OR: U.S. Department of Agriculture, Forest Service, Pacific Northwest Research Station. 277 p.

Westveld, M. 1951. Vegetation mapping as a guide to better silviculture. Ecology. 32(3): 508–517.

Winthers, E.; Fallon, D.; Haglund, J.; DeMeo, T; Nowacki, G.; Tart, D.; Ferwerda, M.; Robertson, G.; Gallegos, A.; Rorick, A.; Cleland, D.T.; Robbie, W. 2005. Terrestrial ecological unit inventory technical guide: landscape and land unit scales. Gen. Tech. Rep. WO-68. Washington, DC: U.S. Department of Agriculture, Forest Service, Washington Office, Ecosystem Management Coordination Staff. 254 p.

Worster, D. 1996. Nature's economy: a history of ecological ideas. 2nd ed. Cambridge, United Kingdom: Cambridge University Press. 507 p.

Zerbe, S. 1998. Potential natural vegetation: validity and applicability in landscape planning and nature conservation. Applied Vegetation Science. 1: 165–172.

Appendix: Potential Vegetation Types of the Blue Mountains Section

Table 8—Potential vegetation types (PVT) of the Blue Mountains section, organized by potential vegetation type code[a]

PVT code (PLANTS code)	PVT common name	Status	Ecoclass	PAG	PVG
ABGR/ACGL	grand fir/Rocky Mountain maple	PA	CWS912	Warm very moist UF	Moist UF
ABGR/ACGL	grand fir/Rocky Mountain maple	PA	CWS541	Warm very moist UF	Moist UF
ABGR/ACGL (FLOODPLAIN)	grand fir/Rocky Mountain maple (floodplain)	PA	CWS543	Warm moderate SM RF	Warm RF
ABGR/ACGL-PHMA5	grand fir/Rocky Mountain maple-mallow ninebark	PCT	CWS412	Warm moist UF	Moist RF
ABGR/ARCO9	grand fir/heartleaf arnica	PCT	CWF444	Cold dry UF	Cold UF
ABGR/ATFI	grand fir/ladyfern	PA	CWF613	Warm high SM RF	Warm RF
ABGR/BRVU	grand fir/Columbia brome	PA	CWG211	Warm moist UF	Moist UF
ABGR/CAGE2	grand fir/elk sedge	PA	CWG111	Warm dry UF	Dry UF
ABGR/CALA30	grand fir/woolly sedge	PC	CWM311	Warm high SM RF	Warm RF
ABGR/CARU	grand fir/pinegrass	PA	CWG112	Warm dry UF	Dry UF
ABGR/CARU	grand fir/pinegrass	PA	CWG113	Warm dry UF	Dry UF
ABGR/CLUN2	grand fir/queencup beadlily	PA	CWF421	Cool moist UF	Moist UF
ABGR/COOC	grand fir/goldthread	PA	CWF511	Cool dry UF	Cold UF
ABGR/CRDO2/CADE9	grand fir/black hawthorn/Dewey's sedge	PA	CWS423	Warm high SM RF	Warm RF
ABGR/GYDR	grand fir/oakfern	PA	CWF611	Cool very moist UF	Moist UF
ABGR/LIBO3	grand fir/twinflower	PA	CWF311	Cool moist UF	Moist UF
ABGR/LIBO3	grand fir/twinflower	PA	CWF312	Cool moist UF	Moist UF
ABGR/POMU-ASCA2	grand fir/swordfern-ginger	PA	CWF612	Cool very moist UF	Moist UF
ABGR/SPBE2	grand fir/birchleaf spiraea	PA	CWS321	Warm dry UF	Dry UF
ABGR/SPBE2	grand fir/birchleaf spiraea	PA	CWS322	Warm dry UF	Dry UF
ABGR/SYAL (FLOODPLAIN)	grand fir/common snowberry (floodplain)	PCT	CWS314	Warm low SM RF	Low SM RF
ABGR/TABR2/CLUN2	grand fir/Pacific yew/queencup beadlily	PA	CWF422	Cool wet UF	Moist UF
ABGR/TABR2/CLUN2	grand fir/Pacific yew/queencup beadlily	PA	CWC811	Cool wet UF	Moist UF
ABGR/TABR2/LIBO3	grand fir/Pacific yew/twinflower	PA	CWC812	Cool wet UF	Moist UF
ABGR/TABR2/LIBO3 (FLOODPLAIN)	grand fir/Pacific yew/twinflower (floodplain)	PA	CWF424	Warm high SM RF	Warm RF
ABGR/TRCA	grand fir/false bugbane	PA	CWF512	Cool very moist UF	Moist UF
ABGR/VAME	grand fir/big huckleberry	PA	CWS211	Cool moist UF	Moist UF
ABGR/VAME	grand fir/big huckleberry	PA	CWS212	Cool moist UF	Moist UF
ABGR/VASC	grand fir/grouse huckleberry	PA	CWS811	Cold dry UF	Cold UF
ABGR/VASC-LIBO3	grand fir/grouse huckleberry-twinflower	PCT	CWS812	Cool moist UF	Moist UF
ABGR-CHNO/VAME	grand fir-Alaska yellow cedar/big huckleberry	PCT	CWS232	Cool moist UF	Moist UF
ABLA/ARCO9	subalpine fir/heartleaf arnica	PA	CEF435	Cool moist UF	Moist UF
ABLA/ARCO9	subalpine fir/heartleaf arnica	PCT	CEF412	Cool moist UF	Moist UF
ABLA/ARNE/ARAC2	subalpine fir/pinemat manzanita/prickly sandwort	PC	CES429	Cool dry UF	Cold UF
ABLA/ATFI	subalpine fir/ladyfern	PA	CEF332	Cold high SM RF	Cold RF
ABLA/CAAQ	subalpine fir/aquatic sedge	PCT	CEM123	Cold high SM RF	Cold RF
ABLA/CACA4	subalpine fir/bluejoint reedgrass	PA	CEM124	Cold moderate SM RF	Cold RF
ABLA/CADI6	subalpine fir/softleaf sedge	PCT	CEM122	Cold high SM RF	Cold RF
ABLA/CAGE2	subalpine fir/elk sedge	PA	CAG111	Cold dry UF	Cold UF
ABLA/CARU	subalpine fir/pinegrass	PA	CEG312	Cool dry UF	Cold UF
ABLA/CLUN2	subalpine fir/queencup beadlily	PA	CES131	Cool moist UF	Moist UF

Table 8—Potential vegetation types (PVT) of the Blue Mountains section, organized by potential vegetation type code[a] (continued)

PVT code (PLANTS code)	PVT common name	Status	Ecoclass	PAG	PVG
ABLA/CLUN2	subalpine fir/queencup beadlily	PA	CES314	Cool moist UF	Moist UF
ABLA/FEVI	subalpine fir/green fescue	PC	CEG411	Cold dry UF	Cold UF
ABLA/JUDR	subalpine fir/Drummond's rush	PC	CEG412	Cold dry UF	Cold UF
ABLA/JUPA (AVALANCHE)	subalpine fir/Parry's rush (avalanche)	PC	CEG414	Cold dry UF	Cold UF
ABLA/JUTE	subalpine fir/slender rush	PC	CEG413	Cold dry UF	Cold UF
ABLA/LIBO3	subalpine fir/twinflower	PA	CEF221	Cool moist UF	Moist UF
ABLA/LIBO3	subalpine fir/twinflower	PA	CES414	Cool moist UF	Moist UF
ABLA/MEFE	subalpine fir/rusty menziesia	PA	CES221	Cold moist UF	Cold UF
ABLA/POPH	subalpine fir/alpine fleeceflower	PC	CEF511	Cold dry UF	Cold UF
ABLA/POPU3	subalpine fir/Jacob's ladder	PA	CEF411	Cold dry UF	Cold UF
ABLA/RHAL2	subalpine fir/white rhododendron	PCT	CES214	Cold moist UF	Cold UF
ABLA/SETR	subalpine fir/arrowleaf groundsel	PA	CEF333	Cold high SM RF	Cold RF
ABLA/STAM2	subalpine fir/claspleaf twistedstalk	PCT	CEF311	Cool wet UF	Moist UF
ABLA/STOC2	subalpine fir/western needlegrass	PCT	CEG323	Cold dry UF	Cold UF
ABLA/TRCA	subalpine fir/false bugbane	PA	CEF331	Cool moist UF	Moist UF
ABLA/VAME	subalpine fir/big huckleberry	PA	CES315	Cool moist UF	Moist UF
ABLA/VAME	subalpine fir/big huckleberry	PA	CES311	Cool moist UF	Moist UF
ABLA/VAME (FLOODPLAIN)	subalpine fir/big huckleberry (floodplain)	PA	CES316	Cold moderate SM RF	Cold RF
ABLA/VASC	subalpine fir/grouse huckleberry	PA	CES411	Cold dry UF	Cold UF
ABLA/VASC/POPU3	subalpine fir/grouse huckleberry/Jacob's ladder	PA	CES415	Cold dry UF	Cold UF
ABLA/VASC-PHEM	subalpine fir/grouse huckleberry-pink mountainheath	PA	CES428	Cold dry UF	Cold UF
ABLA/VAUL/CASC12	subalpine fir/bog blueberry/Holm's Rocky Mountain sedge	PCT	CEM313	Cold high SM RF	Cold RF
ABLA/XETE	subalpine fir/beargrass	PA	CEF111	Cool dry UF	Cold UF
ABLA-PIAL/ARAC2	subalpine fir-whitebark pine/prickly sandwort	PC	CAF324	Cold dry UF	Cold UF
ABLA-PIAL/CAGE2	subalpine fir-whitebark pine/elk sedge	PA	CAG133	Cold dry UF	Cold UF
ABLA-PIAL/FEVI	subalpine fir-whitebark pine/green fescue	PA	CAG222	Cold dry UF	Cold UF
ABLA-PIAL/JUCO6	subalpine fir-whitebark pine/mountain juniper	PC	CAS424	Cold dry UF	Cold UF
ABLA-PIAL/JUCO6-ARNE	subalpine fir-whitebark pine/mountain juniper-pinemat manzanita	PC	CAS423	Cold dry UF	Cold UF
ABLA-PIAL/JUDR	subalpine fir-whitebark pine/Drummond's rush	PCT	CAG3	Cold dry UF	Cold UF
ABLA-PIAL/JUPA-STLE2	subalpine fir-whitebark pine/Parry's rush-Lemmon's needlegrass	PA	CAG132	Cold dry UF	Cold UF
ABLA-PIAL/POPH	subalpine fir-whitebark pine/alpine fleeceflower	PCT	CAF2	Cold dry UF	Cold UF
ABLA-PIAL/POPU3	subalpine fir-whitebark pine/Jacob's ladder	PC	CAF0	Cold dry UF	Cold UF
ABLA-PIAL/RIMO2/POPU3	subalpine fir-whitebark pine/mountain gooseberry/Jacob's ladder	PCT	CAS611	Cold dry UF	Cold UF
ABLA-PIAL/VASC/ARAC2	subalpine fir-whitebark pine/grouse huckleberry/prickly sandwort	PCT	CAS623	Cold dry UF	Cold UF
ABLA-PIAL/VASC/ARCO9	subalpine fir-whitebark pine/grouse huckleberry/heartleaf arnica	PA	CAS621	Cold dry UF	Cold UF
ABLA-PIAL/VASC/CARO5	subalpine fir-whitebark pine/grouse huckleberry/Ross' sedge	PA	CAS622	Cold dry UF	Cold UF
ABLA-PIAL/VASC/FEVI	subalpine fir-whitebark pine/grouse huckleberry/green fescue	PC	CAS625	Cold dry UF	Cold UF
ABLA-PIAL/VASC/FEVI (AVALANCHE)	subalpine fir-whitebark pine/grouse huckleberry/green fescue (avalanche)	PC	CAS629	Cold dry UF	Cold UF
ABLA-PIAL/VASC/LECOW2	subalpine fir-whitebark pine/grouse huckleberry/Wallowa Lewisia	PC	CAS627	Cold dry UF	Cold UF
ABLA-PIAL/VASC/OREX	subalpine fir-whitebark pine/grouse huckleberry/little ricegrass	PC	CAS626	Cold dry UF	Cold UF
ABLA-PIAL/VASC-PHEM	subalpine fir-whitebark pine/grouse huckleberry-pink mountainheath	PCT	CAS624	Cold dry UF	Cold UF
ABLA-PIAL/VASC-PHEM (AVALANCHE)	subalpine fir-whitebark pine/grouse huckleberry-pink mountainheath (avalanche)	PC	CAS628	Cold dry UF	Cold UF
ABLA-PIEN/ARCO9	subalpine fir-Engelmann spruce/heartleaf arnica	PA	CEF436	Cool moist UF	Moist UF
ABLA-PIEN/CLUN2	subalpine fir-Engelmann spruce/queencup beadlily	PA	CEF437	Cool moist UF	Moist UF
ABLA-PIEN/LEGL	subalpine fir-Engelmann spruce/Labrador tea	PA	CES612	Cold moist UF	Cold UF

65

Table 8—Potential vegetation types (PVT) of the Blue Mountains section, organized by potential vegetation type code[a] (continued)

PVT code (PLANTS code)	PVT common name	Status	Ecoclass	PAG	PVG
ABLA-PIEN/LEGL (FLOODPLAIN)	subalpine fir-Engelmann spruce/Labrador tea (floodplain)	PA	CES610	Cold high SM RF	Cold RF
ABLA-PIEN/LIBO3	subalpine fir-Engelmann spruce/twinflower	PC	CEF2	Cool moist UF	Moist UF
ABLA-PIEN/LUHI4	subalpine fir-Engelmann spruce/smooth woodrush	PC	CEG131	Cold dry UF	Cold UF
ABLA-PIEN/MEFE	subalpine fir-Engelmann spruce/rusty menziesia	PA	CES2	Cold moist UF	Cold UF
ABLA-PIEN/MEFE (FLOODPLAIN)	subalpine fir-Engelmann spruce/rusty menziesia (floodplain)	PA	CES710	Cold moderate SM RF	Cold RF
ABLA-PIEN/POPU3	subalpine fir-Engelmann spruce/Jacob's ladder	PC	CEF426	Cold dry UF	Cold UF
ABLA-PIEN/RHAL2	subalpine fir-Engelmann spruce/white rhododendron	PC	CES215	Cold moist UF	Cold UF
ABLA-PIEN/SETR	subalpine fir-Engelmann spruce/arrowleaf groundsel	PC	CEF336	Cold moist UF	Cold UF
ABLA-PIEN/TRCA	subalpine fir-Engelmann spruce/false bugbane	PC	CEF425	Cool moist UF	Moist UF
ABLA-PIEN/VASC-PHEM	subalpine fir-Engelmann spruce/grouse huckleberry-pink mountainheath	PC	CES427	Cold dry UF	Cold UF
ABLA-PIMO3/CHUM	subalpine fir-western white pine/prince's pine	PC	CES8	Cool dry UF	Cold UF
ACGL	Rocky Mountain maple	PCT	HD01	Hot low SM RS	Low SM RS
ADPE	maidenhair fern	PCT	FW4213	Warm high SM RH	Warm RH
AGDI	thin bentgrass	PCT	MD4111	Warm low SM RH	Low SM RH
AGSP-BRCA5	bluebunch wheatgrass-mountain brome	PCT	GB4131	Warm moist UH	Moist UH
AGSP-CYTEF	bluebunch wheatgrass-turpentine cymopterus	PCT	GB4133	Hot dry UH	Dry UH
AGSP-ERHE2	bluebunch wheatgrass-Wyeth's buckwheat	PA	GB4111	Hot dry UH	Dry UH
AGSP-ERUM	bluebunch wheatgrass-sulphurflower buckwheat	PCT	GB4132	Hot dry UH	Dry UH
AGSP-POSA12	bluebunch wheatgrass-Sandberg's bluegrass	PA	GB41	Hot dry UH	Dry UH
AGSP-POSA12	bluebunch wheatgrass-Sandberg's bluegrass	PA	GB4121	Hot dry UH	Dry UH
AGSP-POSA12 (BASALT)	bluebunch wheatgrass-Sandberg's bluegrass (basalt)	PA	GB4113	Hot dry UH	Dry UH
AGSP-POSA12 (GRANITE)	bluebunch wheatgrass-Sandberg's bluegrass (granite)	PA	GB4116	Hot dry UH	Dry UH
AGSP-POSA12-APAN2	bluebunch wheatgrass-Sandberg's bluegrass-spreading dogbane	PA	GB4127	Hot dry UH	Dry UH
AGSP-POSA12-ASCU5	bluebunch wheatgrass-Sandberg's bluegrass-Cusick's milkvetch	PA	GB4114	Hot dry UH	Dry UH
AGSP-POSA12-ASRE5	bluebunch wheatgrass-Sandberg's bluegrass-Blue Mountain milkvetch	PA	GB4125	Hot dry UH	Dry UH
AGSP-POSA12-BASA3	bluebunch wheatgrass-Sandberg's bluegrass-arrowleaf balsamroot	PA	GB4123	Hot dry UH	Dry UH
AGSP-POSA12-DAUN	bluebunch wheatgrass-Sandberg's bluegrass-onespike oatgrass	PA	GB4911	Hot dry UH	Dry UH
AGSP-POSA12-ERHE2	bluebunch wheatgrass-Sandberg's bluegrass-creamy buckwheat	PA	GB4124	Hot dry UH	Dry UH
AGSP-POSA12-ERPU2	bluebunch wheatgrass-Sandberg's bluegrass-shaggy fleabane	PA	GB4115	Hot dry UH	Dry UH
AGSP-POSA12-LUPIN	bluebunch wheatgrass-Sandberg's bluegrass-lupine	PA	GB4119	Hot dry UH	Dry UH
AGSP-POSA12-OPPO	bluebunch wheatgrass-Sandberg's bluegrass-pricklypear	PA	GB4118	Hot dry UH	Dry UH
AGSP-POSA12-PHCO10	bluebunch wheatgrass-Sandberg's bluegrass-Snake River phlox	PA	GB4117	Hot dry UH	Dry UH
AGSP-POSA12-SCAN3	bluebunch wheatgrass-Sandberg's bluegrass-narrowleaf skullcap	PA	GB4112	Hot dry UH	Dry UH
AGSP-POSA12-TRMA3	bluebunch wheatgrass-Sandberg's bluegrass-bighead clover	PA	GB4126	Hot dry UH	Dry UH
AGSP-SPCR-ARLO3	bluebunch wheatgrass-sand dropseed-red threeawn	PCT	GB1911	Hot dry UH	Dry UH
ALIN2/ATFI	mountain alder/ladyfern	PA	SW2116	Warm high SM RS	Warm RS
ALIN2/CAAM10	mountain alder/bigleaf sedge	PA	SW2114	Warm high SM RS	Warm RS
ALIN2/CAAQ	mountain alder/aquatic sedge	PC	SW2126	Warm high SM RS	Warm RS
ALIN2/CACA4	mountain alder/bluejoint reedgrass	PA	SW2121	Warm moderate SM RS	Warm RS
ALIN2/CADE9	mountain alder/Dewey's sedge	PCT	SW2118	Warm moderate SM RS	Warm RS
ALIN2/CALA30	mountain alder/woolly sedge	PA	SW2123	Warm moderate SM RS	Warm RS
ALIN2/CALEL	mountain alder/densely tufted sedge	PC	SW2127	Warm moderate SM RS	Warm RS
ALIN2/CALU7	mountain alder/woodrush sedge	PC	SW2128	Warm low SM RS	Low SM RS
ALIN2/CAUT	mountain alder/bladder sedge	PA	SW2115	Warm high SM RS	Warm RS
ALIN2/EQAR	mountain alder/common horsetail	PA	SW2117	Warm moderate SM RS	Warm RS

Table 8—Potential vegetation types (PVT) of the Blue Mountains section, organized by potential vegetation type code[a] (continued)

PVT code (PLANTS code)	PVT common name	Status	Ecoclass	PAG	PVG
ALIN2/GLEL	mountain alder/tall mannagrass	PA	SW2215	Warm high SM RS	Warm RS
ALIN2/GYDR	mountain alder/oakfern	PCT	SW2125	Warm moderate SM RS	Warm RS
ALIN2/HELA4	mountain alder/common cowparsnip	PCT	SW2124	Warm moderate SM RS	Warm RS
ALIN2/POPR	mountain alder/Kentucky bluegrass	PCT	SW2120	Warm low SM RS	Low SM RS
ALIN2/SCM12	mountain alder/smallfruit bulrush	PCT	SW2122	Warm high SM RS	Warm RS
ALIN2-COST4/MESIC FORB	mountain alder-red osier dogwood/mesic forb	PA	SW2216	Warm moderate SM RS	Warm RS
ALIN2-RIBES/MESIC FORB	mountain alder-currants/mesic forb	PA	SW2217	Warm moderate SM RS	Warm RS
ALIN2-SYAL	mountain alder-common snowberry	PA	SW2211	Warm low SM RS	Low SM RS
ALPR3	meadow foxtail	PCT	MD2111	Warm low SM RH	Low SM RH
ALRH2/MESIC SHRUB	white alder/mesic shrub	PCT	SW2102	Hot moderate SM RF	Warm RF
ALRH2/RUBUS	white alder/blackberry	PCT	SW2101	Hot moderate SM RF	Warm RF
ALRU2 (ALLUVIAL BAR)	red alder (alluvial bar)	PCT	HAF226	Warm moderate SM RF	Warm RF
ALRU2/ATFI	red alder/ladyfern	PCT	HAF227	Warm high SM RF	Warm RF
ALRU2/COST4	red alder/red osier dogwood	PC	HAS511	Warm moderate SM RF	Warm RF
ALRU2/PEFRP	red alder/sweet coltsfoot	PCT	HAF211	Warm moderate SM RF	Warm RF
ALRU2/PHCA11	red alder/Pacific ninebark	PA	HAS211	Warm moderate SM RF	Warm RF
ALRU2/SYAL	red alder/common snowberry	PCT	[none]	Warm moderate SM RF	Warm RF
ALRU2/SYAL/CADE9	red alder/common snowberry/Dewey's sedge	PCT	HAS312	Warm moderate SM RF	Warm RF
ALSI3	Sitka alder snow slides	PCT	SM20	Cold very moist US	Cold US
ALSI3/ATFI	Sitka alder/ladyfern	PA	SW2111	Warm high SM RS	Warm RS
ALSI3/CILA2	Sitka alder/drooping woodreed	PA	SW2112	Warm high SM RS	Warm RS
ALSI3/MESIC FORB	Sitka alder/mesic forb	PCT	SW2113	Warm moderate SM RS	Warm RS
ALVA	Pacific onion	PCT	[none]	Cold high SM RH	Cold RH
ALVA-CASC12	Pacific onion-Holm's Rocky Mountain sedge	PA	FW7111	Cold high SM RH	Cold RH
AMAL2	western serviceberry	PCT	SW3114	Hot low SM RS	Low SM RS
ARAR8/AGSP	low sagebrush/bluebunch wheatgrass	PA	SD1924	Warm dry US	Dry US
ARAR8/FEID-AGSP	low sagebrush/Idaho fescue-bluebunch wheatgrass	PA	SD1911	Warm moist US	Moist US
ARAR8/POSA12	low sagebrush/Sandberg's bluegrass	PA	SD9221	Warm dry US	Dry US
ARCA13/DECE	silver sagebrush/tufted hairgrass	PA	SW6111	Hot moderate SM RS	Warm RS
ARCA13/POCU3	silver sagebrush/Cusick's bluegrass	PCT	SW6114	Hot low SM RS	Low SM RS
ARCA13/POPR	silver sagebrush/Kentucky bluegrass	PCT	SW6112	Hot low SM RS	Low SM RS
ARLU	white sagebrush	PCT	SD01	Warm low SM RH	Low SM RH
ARRI2/PEGA	stiff sagebrush/Gairdner's penstemon	PCT	SD9141	Warm dry US	Dry US
ARRI2/POSA12 (SCAB)	stiff sagebrush/Sandberg's bluegrass (scabland)	PA	SD9111	Warm dry US	Dry US
ARTR4/POSA12-DAUN	threetip sagebrush/Sandberg's bluegrass-onespike oatgrass	PCT	SD2401	Warm dry US	Dry US
ARTRV/AGSP-POSA12	mountain big sagebrush/bluebunch wheatgrass-Sandberg's bluegrass	PA	SD2918	Warm dry US	Dry US
ARTRV/BRCA5	mountain big sagebrush/mountain brome	PCT	SS4914	Warm moist US	Moist US
ARTRV/CAGE2	mountain big sagebrush/elk sedge	PA	SS4911	Cold moist US	Cold US
ARTRV/CAGE2 (MONTANE)	mountain big sagebrush/elk sedge (montane)	PCT	SD2915	Warm moist US	Moist US
ARTRV/CAHO5	mountain big sagebrush/Hood's sedge	PCT	SS4916	Cold moist US	Cold US
ARTRV/ELCI2	mountain big sagebrush/basin wildrye	PCT	SD3011	Warm moist US	Moist US
ARTRV/ERFL4-PHLOX	mountain big sagebrush/golden buckwheat-phlox	PC	SS4918	Cool dry US	Cold US
ARTRV/FEID-AGSP	mountain big sagebrush/Idaho fescue-bluebunch wheatgrass	PA	SD2911	Warm moist US	Moist US
ARTRV/FEID-KOCR	mountain big sagebrush/Idaho fescue-prairie junegrass	PA	SD2929	Warm moist US	Moist US
ARTRV/FEVI	mountain big sagebrush/green fescue	PCT	SS4915	Cold moist US	Cold US

Table 8—Potential vegetation types (PVT) of the Blue Mountains section, organized by potential vegetation type code[a](continued)

PVT code (PLANTS code)	PVT common name	Status	Ecoclass	PAG	PVG
ARTRV/LINU4	mountain big sagebrush/linanthus	PCT	SS4917	Cool dry US	Cold US
ARTRV/POCU3	mountain big sagebrush/Cusick's bluegrass	PA	SW6113	Hot low SM RS	Low SM RS
ARTRV/STOC2	mountain big sagebrush/western needlegrass	PC	SD2920	Cool dry US	Cold US
ARTRV-PERA4	mountain big sagebrush-squaw apple	PCT	SD3010	Warm moist US	Moist US
ARTRV-PUTR2/FEID	mountain big sagebrush-bitterbrush/Idaho fescue	PCT	SD2916	Hot moist US	Moist US
ARTRV-SYOR2	mountain big sagebrush-mountain snowberry	PCT	SD2919	Warm moist US	Moist US
ARTRV-SYOR2/BRCA5	mountain big sagebrush-mountain snowberry/mountain brome	PCT	SD2917	Warm moist US	Moist US
BEOC2/MESIC FORB	water birch/mesic forb	PCT	SW3112	Warm moderate SM RS	Warm RS
BEOC2/PHAR3	water birch/reed canarygrass	PC	SM41	Warm moderate SM RS	Warm RS
BEOC2/WET SEDGE	water birch/wet sedge	PCT	SW3113	Warm high SM RS	Warm RS
BERE/AGSP-APAN2	creeping Oregongrape/bluebunch wheatgrass-spreading dogbane	PCT	GB4915	Warm dry US	Dry US
CAAM10	bigleaf sedge	PA	MM2921	Warm high SM RH	Warm RH
CAAQ	aquatic sedge	PA	MM2914	Cool high SM RH	Cold RH
CACA11	silvery sedge	PCT	MS3113	Warm moderate SM RH	Warm RH
CACA4	bluejoint reedgrass	PA	GM4111	Cool moderate SM RH	Cold RH
CACU2 (SEEP)	Cusick's camas (seep)	PCT	FW3911	Warm very moist UH	Moist UH
CACU5	Cusick's sedge	PA	MM2918	Warm high SM RH	Warm RH
CAEU2	widefruit sedge	PA	MM2913	Cold high SM RH	Cold RH
CAGE2-CARU	elk sedge-pinegrass	PC	GS3914	Cold dry UH	Cold UH
CAGE2-FEID	elk sedge-Idaho fescue	PC	GS3912	Cold dry UH	Cold UH
CAGE2-JUPA	elk sedge-Parry's rush	PC	GS3913	Cold dry UH	Cold UH
CAGE2-PHAU3	elk sedge-desert phlox	PC	GS3916	Cold dry UH	Cold UH
CAGE2-POCU3	elk sedge-Cusick's bluegrass	PC	GS3915	Cold dry UH	Cold UH
CAGE2-STOC2	elk sedge-western needlegrass	PC	GS3917	Cold dry UH	Cold UH
CAHO5	Hood's sedge	PCT	GS64	Cool moist UH	Cold UH
CAHO5-BRCA5	Hood's sedge-mountain brome	PC	GS61	Cool moist UH	Cold UH
CAHO5-BRCA5 (MEADOW)	Hood's sedge-mountain brome (meadow)	PC	GS4012	Cool moist UH	Cold UH
CAHO5-CAGE2	Hood's sedge-elk sedge	PC	GS62	Cool moist UH	Cold UH
CAHO5-POGL9	Hood's sedge-sticky cinquefoil	PC	GS63	Cool dry UH	Cold UH
CAJO	Jones' sedge	PC	MM2933	Warm moderate SM RH	Warm RH
CALA11	slender sedge	PA	MM2920	Warm high SM RH	Warm RH
CALA13	smoothstemmed sedge	PC	MW2913	Cold high SM RH	Cold RH
CALA30	woolly sedge	PA	MM2911	Warm moderate SM RH	Warm RH
CALE8	lakeshore sedge	PA	MM2919	Warm moderate SM RH	Warm RH
CALE9	Sierra hare sedge	PA	MM2927	Cold high SM RH	Cold RH
CALI7	mud sedge	PA	MM2928	Cold high SM RH	Cold RH
CALU7	woodrush sedge	PA	MM2916	Cold high SM RH	Cold RH
CAMI7	smallwing sedge	PCT	MM2929	Warm moderate SM RH	Warm RH
CAMU7	star sedge	PCT	MS3112	Warm moderate SM RH	Warm RH
CANE2	Nebraska sedge	PCT	MM2912	Warm moderate SM RH	Warm RH
CANI2	black alpine sedge	PA	MS2111	Cold moderate SM RH	Cold RH
CANU5	torrent sedge	PCT	MM2922	Hot high SM RH	Warm RH
CAPR5	clustered field sedge	PCT	MW2912	Cold high SM RH	Cold RH
CAREX-STOC2	alpine sedges-western needlegrass	PC	GS4011	Cold dry UH	Cold UH

Table 8—Potential vegetation types (PVT) of the Blue Mountains section, organized by potential vegetation type code[a] (continued)

PVT code (PLANTS code)	PVT common name	Status	Ecoclass	PAG	PVG
CASC10-SAAR13	northern singlespike sedge-brook saxifrage	PA	MS2113	Cold high SM RH	Cold RH
CASC12	Holm's Rocky Mountain sedge	PA	MS3111	Cold high SM RH	Cold RH
CASH	Sheldon's sedge	PCT	MM2932	Hot moderate SM RH	Warm RH
CASI2	shortbeaked sedge	PCT	MM2915	Warm high SM RH	Warm RH
CAST5	sawbeak sedge	PCT	MW1926	Warm high SM RH	Warm RH
CASU6	brown sedge	PC	MM2930	Warm moderate SM RH	Warm RH
CAUT	bladder sedge	PA	MM2917	Cool high SM RH	Cold RH
CAVE6	inflated sedge	PA	MW1923	Cool high SM RH	Cold RH
CELE3	mountain mahogany	PCT	SD49	Warm dry US	Dry US
CELE3/AGSP	mountain mahogany/bluebunch wheatgrass	PCT	SD4112	Warm dry US	Dry US
CELE3/CAGE2	mountain mahogany/elk sedge	PC	SD40	Warm moist US	Moist US
CELE3/CAGE2	mountain mahogany/elk sedge	PC	SD4113	Warm moist US	Moist US
CELE3/FEID-AGSP	mountain mahogany/Idaho fescue-bluebunch wheatgrass	PA	SD4111	Warm moist US	Moist US
CELE3/PONEW	mountain mahogany/Wheeler's bluegrass	PCT	SD4114	Warm dry US	Dry US
CELE3-PUTR2/AGSP	mountain mahogany-bitterbrush/bluebunch wheatgrass	PCT	SD4115	Warm moist US	Moist US
CERE2/AGSP	netleaf hackberry/bluebunch wheatgrass	PA	SD5611	Hot moist US	Moist US
CERE2/BROMU	netleaf hackberry/brome	PCT	SD5612	Hot low SM RS	Low SM RS
CEVE	snowbrush ceanothus	PCT	SM33	Warm moist US	Moist US
CILA2	drooping woodreed	PC	MW2927	Cold high SM RH	Cold RH
COST4	red osier dogwood	PA	SW5112	Warm moderate SM RS	Warm RS
COST4/ATFI	red osier dogwood/ladyfern	PA	SW4133	Warm high SM RS	Warm RS
COST4/SAAR13	red osier dogwood/brook saxifrage	PCT	SW5118	Warm high SM RS	Warm RS
CRDO2/MESIC FORB	black hawthorn/mesic forb	PCT	SW3111	Hot low SM RS	Low SM RS
DAUN-LOLE2	onespike oatgrass-slenderfruit lomatium	PA	GB9114	Hot moist UH	Moist UH
DECE	tufted hairgrass	PA	MM1912	Cool moderate SM RH	Cold RH
ELBE	delicate spikerush	PC	MS4111	Cold high SM RH	Cold RH
ELCI2	basin wildrye	PCT	GB7111	Hot very moist UH	Moist UH
ELPA3	creeping spikerush	PA	MW4912	Hot high SM RH	Warm RH
ELPA6	fewflowered spikerush	PA	MW4911	Cold high SM RH	Cold RH
EQAR	common horsetail	PA	FW4212	Warm moderate SM RH	Warm RH
ERDO-POSA12	Douglas' buckwheat-Sandberg's bluegrass	PCT	FM9111	Hot dry UH	Dry UH
ERFL4-PECO	golden buckwheat-coiled lousewort	PC	FS8116	Cool dry UH	Cold UH
ERIOG-PHOR2	buckwheat/Oregon bladderpod	PA	SD9322	Hot dry UH	Dry UH
ERST4-POSA12	strict buckwheat/Sandberg's bluegrass	PCT	FM9112	Hot dry UH	Dry UH
ERUM (RIDGE)	sulphurflower (ridge)	PCT	FM9113	Hot dry UH	Dry UH
FEID (ALPINE)	Idaho fescue (alpine)	PCT	GS12	Cold moist UH	Cold UH
FEID-AGSP	Idaho fescue-bluebunch wheatgrass	PA	GB59	Warm moist UH	Moist UH
FEID-AGSP (RIDGE)	Idaho fescue-bluebunch wheatgrass (ridge)	PCT	GB5915	Warm moist UH	Moist UH
FEID-AGSP-BASA3	Idaho fescue-bluebunch wheatgrass-arrowleaf balsamroot	PA	GB5917	Warm moist UH	Moist UH
FEID-AGSP-CYTEF	Idaho fescue-bluebunch wheatgrass-cymopterus	PA	GB5925	Warm dry UH	Dry UH
FEID-AGSP-FRALC2	Idaho fescue-bluebunch wheatgrass-Cusick's frasera	PA	GB5926	Cool moist UH	Cold UH
FEID-AGSP-LUPIN	Idaho fescue-bluebunch wheatgrass-lupine	PA	GB5916	Warm moist UH	Moist UH
FEID-AGSP-PHCO10	Idaho fescue-bluebunch wheatgrass-Snake River phlox	PA	GB5918	Warm moist UH	Moist UH
FEID-AGSP-PHLOX	Idaho fescue-bluebunch wheatgrass-phlox	PA	GB5931	Warm moist UH	Moist UH
FEID-AGSP-PONEW	Idaho fescue-bluebunch wheatgrass-Wheeler's bluegrass	PC	GB5927	Warm dry UH	Dry UH

69

Table 8—Potential vegetation types (PVT) of the Blue Mountains section, organized by potential vegetation type code[a] (continued)

PVT code (PLANTS code)	PVT common name	Status	Ecoclass	PAG	PVG
FEID-CAGE2	Idaho fescue-elk sedge	PCT	GB5922	Warm moist UH	Moist UH
FEID-CAHO5	Idaho fescue-Hood's sedge	PA	GB5921	Warm moist UH	Moist UH
FEID-DAIN-CAPE7	Idaho fescue-timber oatgrass-Liddon's sedge	PA	GB5920	Warm very moist UH	Moist UH
FEID-DAUN	Idaho Fescue-onespike oatgrass	PCT	GB5932	Warm dry UH	Dry UH
FEID-GETR	Idaho fescue-red avens	PCT	GB5923	Cool moist UH	Cold UH
FEID-KOCR (HIGH)	Idaho fescue-prairie junegrass (high elevation)	PA	GB5913	Cool moist UH	Cold UH
FEID-KOCR (LOW)	Idaho fescue-prairie junegrass (low elevation)	PA	GB5914	Warm moist UH	Moist UH
FEID-KOCR (MOUND)	Idaho fescue-prairie junegrass (mound)	PA	GB5912	Cool moist UH	Cold UH
FEID-KOCR (RIDGE)	Idaho fescue-prairie junegrass (ridge)	PA	GB5911	Cool moist UH	Cold UH
FEID-PESP2	Idaho fescue-Wallowa penstemon	PCT	GB5924	Cool moist UH	Cold UH
FELLFIELD	fellfield	PC	GS60	Cold dry UH	Cold UH
FESC-FEID	rough fescue-Idaho fescue	PC	GB6011	Cold dry UH	Cold UH
FEVI	green fescue	PA	GS11	Cold moist UH	Cold UH
FEVI-AGCA2	green fescue-bearded wheatgrass	PC	GS1118	Cold moist UH	Cold UH
FEVI-CAHO5	green fescue-Hood's sedge	PCT	GS1111	Cold moist UH	Cold UH
FEVI-CARO5	green fescue-Ross' sedge	PCT	GS1114	Cold moist UH	Cold UH
FEVI-CASC12	green fescue-Holm's Rocky Mountain sedge	PC	GS1119	Cold moist UH	Cold UH
FEVI-JUPA	green fescue-Parry's rush	PA	GS1113	Cold dry UH	Cold UH
FEVI-LICA2	green fescue-Canby's lovage	PC	GS1117	Cold moist UH	Cold UH
FEVI-LULA3	green fescue-spurred lupine	PC	GS1112	Cold moist UH	Cold UH
FEVI-PENST	green fescue-penstemon	PCT	GS1115	Cold moist UH	Cold UH
FEVI-STOC2	green fescue-western needlegrass	PCT	GS1116	Cold moist UH	Cold UH
GLEL	tall mannagrass	PA	MM2925	Warm high SM RH	Warm RH
GLSPA/AGSP	spiny greasebush/bluebunch wheatgrass	PA	SD65	Hot dry US	Dry US
GRUS	grus	PC	FS92	Cold dry UH	Cold UH
HELA4-ELGL	common cowparsnip/blue wildrye	PC	SW3124	Warm moderate SM RH	Warm RH
JUBA	Baltic rush	PCT	MW3912	Warm moderate SM RH	Warm RH
JUCO6	mountain juniper	PC	CJC1	Warm moist US	Moist US
JUOC/AGSP	western juniper/bluebunch wheatgrass	PCT	CJG113	Hot dry UW	Dry UW
JUOC/ARAR8	western juniper/low sagebrush	PCT	CJS1	Hot dry UW	Dry UW
JUOC/ARAR8/FEID	western juniper/low sagebrush/Idaho fescue	PA	CJS112	Hot dry UW	Dry UW
JUOC/ARRI2	western juniper/stiff sagebrush	PCT	CJS8	Hot dry UW	Dry UW
JUOC/ARRI2 (SCAB)	western juniper/stiff sagebrush (scabland)	PCT	CJS811	Hot dry UW	Dry UW
JUOC/ARTRV/FEID-AGSP	western juniper/mountain big sagebrush/Idaho fescue-bluebunch wheatgrass	PCT	CJS2	Hot moist UW	Moist UW
JUOC/CELE3/CAGE2	western juniper/mountain mahogany/elk sedge	PCT	CJS42	Hot moist UW	Moist UW
JUOC/CELE3/FEID-AGSP	western juniper/mountain mahogany/Idaho fescue-bluebunch wheatgrass	PA	CJS41	Hot moist UW	Moist UW
JUOC/FEID-AGSP	western juniper/Idaho fescue-bluebunch wheatgrass	PA	CJG111	Hot moist UW	Moist UW
JUOC/PUTR2/FEID-AGSP	western juniper/bitterbrush/Idaho fescue-bluebunch wheatgrass	PA	CJS321	Hot moist UW	Moist UW
JUPA-AGGL	Parry's rush-pale agoseris	PC	GS4013	Cold dry UH	Cold UH
JUSC2/CELE3	Rocky Mountain juniper-mountain mahogany	PC	CJS5	Warm dry UF	Dry UF
KAMI/CANI2	alpine laurel/black alpine sedge	PA	SW901	Cold high SM RS	Cold RS
LECOW2 (RIM)	Wallowa Lewisia (rim)	PCT	FX4111	Hot dry UH	Dry UH
LEGL/CASC12	Labrador tea/Holm's Rocky Mountain sedge	PC	SW0101	Cold moderate SM RS	Cold RS
LEPY2-MAGL2	pygmy Lewisia-cluster tarweed	PC	FS8113	Cool moist UH	Cold UH
LINU4-ARLO6	linanthus-longleaf arnica	PC	FS8115	Cool moist UH	Cold UH

70

Table 8—Potential vegetation types (PVT) of the Blue Mountains section, organized by potential vegetation type code[a] (continued)

PVT code (PLANTS code)	PVT common name	Status	Ecoclass	PAG	PVG
LINU4-ARLU	linanthus–white sagebrush	PC	FS80	Cool dry UH	Cold UH
LINU4-CYTEF	linanthus–cymopterus	PC	FS1113	Cool dry UH	Cold UH
LOIN5/ATFI	twinberry honeysuckle/ladyfern	PC	SW0102	Warm moderate SM RS	Warm RS
MEBU-STOC2	oniongrass–western needlegrass	PCT	GB5011	Warm dry UH	Dry UH
METR3	buckbean	PC	FW6111	Warm high SM RH	Warm RH
MOOD	mountain balm	PC	FS8112	Cool dry UH	Cold UH
NUPO2	Rocky Mountain pondlily	PA	MT10	Cool high SM RH	Cold RH
PERA4-SYOR2	squaw apple–mountain snowberry	PCT	SD30	Hot moist US	Moist US
PHCA11	Pacific ninebark	PC	SM1901	Warm low SM RS	Low SM RS
PHEM (MOUNDS)	pink mountainheath (mounds)	PA	SS1912	Cold moderate SM RS	Cold RS
PHLE4 (TALUS)	syringa-bordered talus strips	PCT	NTS111	Hot very moist US	Moist US
PHLE4/MESIC FORB	Lewis' mockorange/mesic forb	PCT	SM3001	Hot low SM RS	Low SM RS
PHLOX-CYTEF	phlox-cymopteris	PC	FS8117	Cold dry UH	Cold UH
PHLOX-IVGO	phlox-Ivesia	PC	FS8118	Cold dry UH	Cold UH
PHMA5-SYAL	mallow ninebark–common snowberry	PCT	SM19	Warm moist US	Moist US
PHMA5-SYAL	mallow ninebark–common snowberry	PCT	SM1111	Warm moist US	Moist US
PIAL/ARAC2	whitebark pine/prickly sandwort	PCT	CAF322	Cold dry UF	Cold UF
PIAL/CAGE2	whitebark pine/elk sedge	PA	CAG131	Cold dry UF	Cold UF
PIAL/FEVI	whitebark pine/green fescue	PA	CAG221	Cold dry UF	Cold UF
PIAL/JUCO6-ARNE	whitebark pine/mountain juniper-pinemat manzanita	PC	CAS422	Cold dry UF	Cold UF
PIAL/LUAR3	whitebark pine/silvery lupine	PC	CAF323	Cold dry UF	Cold UF
PIAL/RIMO2/POPU3	whitebark pine/mountain gooseberry/Jacob's ladder	PA	CAS512	Cold dry UF	Cold UF
PIAL/VASC/ARAC2	whitebark pine/grouse huckleberry/prickly sandwort	PC	CAS313	Cold dry UF	Cold UF
PIAL/VASC/ARCO9	whitebark pine/grouse huckleberry/heartleaf arnica	PC	CAS312	Cold dry UF	Cold UF
PIAL/VASC/LUHI4	whitebark pine/grouse huckleberry/smooth woodrush	PA	CAS311	Cold dry UF	Cold UF
PICO(ABGR)/ALSI3	lodgepole pine(grand fir)/Sitka alder	PCT	CLS58	Cool very moist UF	Moist UF
PICO(ABGR)/ARNE	lodgepole pine(grand fir)/pinemat manzanita	PCT	CLS57	Cool dry UF	Cold UF
PICO(ABGR)/CARU	lodgepole pine(grand fir)/pinegrass	PCT	CLG21	Cool dry UF	Cold UF
PICO(ABGR)/LIBO3	lodgepole pine(grand fir)/twinflower	PCT	CLF211	Cool moist UF	Moist UF
PICO(ABGR)/VAME	lodgepole pine(grand fir)/big huckleberry	PCT	CLS513	Cool moist UF	Moist UF
PICO(ABGR)/VAME/CARU	lodgepole pine(grand fir)/big huckleberry/pinegrass	PCT	CLS512	Cool moist UF	Moist UF
PICO(ABGR)/VAME/PTAQ	lodgepole pine(grand fir)/big huckleberry/bracken fern	PCT	CLS519	Cool moist UF	Moist UF
PICO(ABGR)/VAME-LIBO3	lodgepole pine(grand fir)/big huckleberry/twinflower	PCT	CLS5	Cool moist UF	Moist UF
PICO(ABGR)/VASC/CARU	lodgepole pine(grand fir)/grouse huckleberry/pinegrass	PCT	CLS417	Cold dry UF	Cold UF
PICO(ABLA)/CAGE2	lodgepole pine(subalpine fir)/elk sedge	PCT	CLG322	Cold dry UF	Cold UF
PICO(ABLA)/STOC2	lodgepole pine(subalpine fir)/western needlegrass	PCT	CLG11	Cold dry UF	Cold UF
PICO(ABLA)/VAME	lodgepole pine(subalpine fir)/big huckleberry	PCT	CLS515	Cool moist UF	Moist UF
PICO(ABLA)/VAME	lodgepole pine(subalpine fir)/big huckleberry	PCT	CLS514	Cool moist UF	Moist UF
PICO(ABLA)/VAME/CARU	lodgepole pine(subalpine fir)/big huckleberry/pinegrass	PCT	CLS516	Cool moist UF	Moist UF
PICO(ABLA)/VASC	lodgepole pine(subalpine fir)/grouse huckleberry	PCT	CLS418	Cold dry UF	Cold UF
PICO(ABLA)/VASC/POPU3	lodgepole pine(subalpine fir)/grouse huckleberry/Jacob's ladder	PCT	CLS415	Cold dry UF	Cold UF
PICO/ALIN2/MESIC FORB	lodgepole pine/mountain alder/mesic forb	PC	CLM511	Cold moderate SM RF	Cold RF
PICO/CAAQ	lodgepole pine/aquatic sedge	PA	CLM114	Cold high SM RF	Cold RF
PICO/CACA4	lodgepole pine/bluejoint reedgrass	PC	CLM117	Cold moderate SM RF	Cold RF
PICO/CALA30	lodgepole pine/woolly sedge	PC	CLM116	Cold moderate SM RF	Cold RF

71

Table 8—Potential vegetation types (PVT) of the Blue Mountains section, organized by potential vegetation type code[a] (continued)

PVT code (PLANTS code)	PVT common name	Status	Ecoclass	PAG	PVG
PICO/CARU	lodgepole pine/pinegrass	PA	CLS416	Cool dry UF	Cold UF
PICO/CASC12	lodgepole pine/Holm's Rocky Mountain sedge	PC	CLM118	Cold high SM RF	Cold RF
PICO/DECE	lodgepole pine/tufted hairgrass	PA	CLM115	Cold moderate SM RF	Cold RF
PICO/POPR	lodgepole pine/Kentucky bluegrass	PCT	CLM112	Cold low SM RF	Cold RF
PIEN/ATFI	Engelmann spruce/ladyfern	PCT	CEF334	Cold high SM RF	Cold RF
PIEN/BRVU	Engelmann spruce/Columbia brome	PCT	CEM125	Cold low SM RF	Cold RF
PIEN/CADI6	Engelmann spruce/softleaf sedge	PA	CEM121	Cold high SM RF	Cold RF
PIEN/CILA2	Engelmann spruce/drooping woodreed	PC	CEM126	Cold moderate SM RF	Cold RF
PIEN/COST4	Engelmann spruce/red osier dogwood	PA	CES511	Cold moderate SM RF	Cold RF
PIEN/EQAR	Engelmann spruce/common horsetail	PA	CEM211	Cold moderate SM RF	Cold RF
PIEN/SETR	Engelmann spruce/arrowleaf groundsel	PA	CEF335	Cold high SM RF	Cold RF
PIEN-ABLA/CASC12	Engelmann spruce-subalpine fir/Holm's Rocky Mountain sedge	PA	CEG201	Cold high SM RF	Cold RF
PIEN-ABLA/SETR	Engelmann spruce-subalpine fir/arrowleaf groundsel	PA	CEM201	Cold high SM RF	Cold RF
PIFL2/JUCO6	limber pine/mountain juniper	PCT	CAS511	Cold dry UF	Cold UF
PIMO3/DECE	western white pine/tufted hairgrass	PCT	CQM111	Warm moderate SM RF	Warm RF
PIPO/AGSP	ponderosa pine/bluebunch wheatgrass	PA	CPG132	Hot dry UF	Dry UF
PIPO/AGSP	ponderosa pine/bluebunch wheatgrass	PA	CPG111	Hot dry UF	Dry UF
PIPO/ARAR8	ponderosa pine/low sagebrush	PCT	CPS61	Hot moist UF	Dry UF
PIPO/ARTRV/CAGE2	ponderosa pine/mountain big sagebrush/elk sedge	PCT	CPS132	Hot dry UF	Dry UF
PIPO/ARTRV/FEID-AGSP	ponderosa pine/mountain big sagebrush/Idaho fescue-bluebunch wheatgrass	PA	CPS131	Hot dry UF	Dry UF
PIPO/CAGE2	ponderosa pine/elk sedge	PA	CPG222	Warm dry UF	Dry UF
PIPO/CARU	ponderosa pine/pinegrass	PA	CPG221	Warm dry UF	Dry UF
PIPO/CELE3/CAGE2	ponderosa pine/mountain mahogany/elk sedge	PA	CPS232	Warm dry UF	Dry UF
PIPO/CELE3/FEID-AGSP	ponderosa pine/mountain mahogany/Idaho fescue-bluebunch wheatgrass	PA	CPS234	Hot dry UF	Dry UF
PIPO/CELE3/PONEW	ponderosa pine/mountain mahogany/Wheeler's bluegrass	PA	CPS233	Hot dry UF	Dry UF
PIPO/CRDO2	ponderosa pine/black hawthorn	PC	CPS722	Hot moderate SM RF	Warm RF
PIPO/FEID	ponderosa pine/Idaho fescue	PA	CPG131	Hot dry UF	Dry UF
PIPO/FEID	ponderosa pine/Idaho fescue	PA	CPG112	Hot dry UF	Dry UF
PIPO/PERA4	ponderosa pine/squaw apple	PCT	CPS8	Hot dry UF	Dry UF
PIPO/POPR	ponderosa pine/Kentucky bluegrass	PCT	CPM112	Hot low SM RF	Low SM RF
PIPO/PUTR2/AGSP	ponderosa pine/bitterbrush/bluebunch wheatgrass	PA	CPS231	Hot dry UF	Dry UF
PIPO/PUTR2/AGSP-POSA12	ponderosa pine/bitterbrush/bluebunch wheatgrass-Sandberg's bluegrass	PA	CPS229	Hot dry UF	Dry UF
PIPO/PUTR2/CAGE2	ponderosa pine/bitterbrush/elk sedge	PA	CPS222	Warm dry UF	Dry UF
PIPO/PUTR2/CARO5	ponderosa pine/bitterbrush/Ross' sedge	PA	CPS221	Warm dry UF	Dry UF
PIPO/PUTR2/FEID-AGSP	ponderosa pine/bitterbrush/Idaho fescue-bluebunch wheatgrass	PA	CPS226	Hot dry UF	Dry UF
PIPO/RHGL	ponderosa pine/smooth sumac	PCT	CPS9	Hot dry UF	Dry UF
PIPO/SPBE2	ponderosa pine/birchleaf spiraea	PCT	CPS523	Warm dry UF	Dry UF
PIPO/SYAL	ponderosa pine/common snowberry	PA	CPS524	Warm dry UF	Dry UF
PIPO/SYAL	ponderosa pine/common snowberry	PA	CPS522	Warm dry UF	Dry UF
PIPO/SYAL (FLOODPLAIN)	ponderosa pine/common snowberry (floodplain)	PA	CPS511	Hot low SM RF	Low SM RF
PIPO/SYOR2	ponderosa pine/mountain snowberry	PA	CPS525	Warm dry UF	Dry UF
PIPO-JUOC/CELE3-SYOR2	ponderosa pine-western juniper/mountain mahogany-mountain snowberry	PCT	CPC212	Hot dry UF	Dry UF
POBU-MAGL2	bulbous bluegrass-cluster tarweed	PCT	GB4411	Hot dry UH	Dry UH
POFR4	shrubby cinquefoil	PC	SS60	Cool moist US	Cold US
POFR4/DECE	shrubby cinquefoil/tufted hairgrass	PA	SW5113	Warm moderate SM RS	Warm RS
POFR4/FEID	shrubby cinquefoil/Idaho fescue	PCT	SS4919	Warm moist US	Moist US

72

Table 8—Potential vegetation types (PVT) of the Blue Mountains section, organized by potential vegetation type code[a] (continued)

PVT code (PLANTS code)	PVT common name	Status	Ecoclass	PAG	PVG
POFR4/POPR	shrubby cinquefoil/Kentucky bluegrass	PCT	SW5114	Warm low SM RS	Low SM RS
POFR4-BEGL	shrubby cinquefoil-bog birch	PCT	SS6001	Cold moderate SM RS	Cold RS
POPH (CORNICES)	alpine fleeceflower (cornices)	PC	FS5916	Cold moist UH	Cold UH
POPH-AGUR-LINU4	alpine fleeceflower-horsemint-linanthus	PC	FS5915	Cool dry UH	Cold UH
POPH-CAGE2-LINU4	alpine fleeceflower-elk sedge-linanthus	PC	FS5914	Cool dry UH	Cold UH
POPH-CARU-CAGE2	alpine fleeceflower-pinegrass-elk sedge	PC	FS5913	Cool dry UH	Cold UH
POPH-FEVI	alpine fleeceflower-green fescue	PC	FS5912	Cold moist UH	Cold UH
POPR (DEGEN BENCH)	Kentucky bluegrass (degenerated bench)	PCT	MD3112	Cool moist UH	Cold UH
POPR (DRY MEADOW)	Kentucky bluegrass (dry meadow)	PCT	MD3111	Warm low SM RH	Low SM RH
POSA12-DAUN	Sandberg's bluegrass-onespike oatgrass	PA	GB9111	Hot dry UH	Dry UH
POSA12-SELA	Sandberg's bluegrass-lanceleaf stonecrop	PC	GB9112	Warm dry UH	Dry UH
POTR15/ACGL	black cottonwood/Rocky Mountain maple	PCT	HCS114	Warm moderate SM RF	Warm RF
POTR15/ALIN2-COST4	black cottonwood/mountain alder-red osier dogwood	PA	HCS113	Warm moderate SM RF	Warm RF
POTR15/SALA5	black cottonwood/Pacific willow	PA	HCS112	Hot moderate SM RF	Warm RF
POTR15/SYAL	black cottonwood/common snowberry	PCT	HCS311	Hot moderate SM RF	Warm RF
POTR15/SYAL	black cottonwood/common snowberry	PCT	HCS312	Hot moderate SM RF	Warm RF
POTR5/ALIN2-COST4	quaking aspen/mountain alder-red osier dogwood	PCT	HQS222	Warm moderate SM RF	Warm RF
POTR5/ALIN2-SYAL	quaking aspen/mountain alder-common snowberry	PCT	HQS223	Warm moderate SM RF	Warm RF
POTR5/CAAQ	quaking aspen/aquatic sedge	PCT	HQM212	Warm high SM RF	Warm RF
POTR5/CACA4	quaking aspen/bluejoint reedgrass	PCT	HQM123	Warm moderate SM RF	Warm RF
POTR5/CAGE2	quaking aspen/elk sedge	PC	HQG112	Cool very moist UF	Moist UF
POTR5/CALA30	quaking aspen/woolly sedge	PA	HQM211	Warm moderate SM RF	Warm RF
POTR5/MESIC FORB	quaking aspen/mesic forb	PCT	HQM511	Warm moderate SM RF	Warm RF
POTR5/POPR	quaking aspen/Kentucky bluegrass	PCT	HQM122	Hot low SM RF	Low SM RF
POTR5/SYAL	quaking aspen/common snowberry	PCT	HQS221	Hot moderate SM RF	Warm RF
PREM	bitter cherry	PC	SM34	Warm moist US	Moist US
PSME/ACGL-PHMA5	Douglas-fir/Rocky Mountain maple-mallow ninebark	PA	CDS722	Warm moist UF	Moist UF
PSME/ACGL-PHMA5 (FLOODPLAIN)	Douglas-fir/Rocky Mountain maple-mallow ninebark (floodplain)	PA	CDS724	Warm moderate SM RF	Warm RF
PSME/ACGL-SYOR2	Douglas-fir/Rocky Mountain maple-mountain snowberry	PC	CDS725	Warm moist UF	Moist UF
PSME/ARNE/CAGE2	Douglas-fir/pinemat manzanita/elk sedge	PA	CDS664	Warm dry UF	Dry UF
PSME/CAGE2	Douglas-fir/elk sedge	PA	CDG111	Warm dry UF	Dry UF
PSME/CARU	Douglas-fir/pinegrass	PA	CDG121	Warm dry UF	Dry UF
PSME/CARU	Douglas-fir/pinegrass	PA	CDG112	Warm dry UF	Dry UF
PSME/CELE3/CAGE2	Douglas-fir/mountain mahogany/elk sedge	PCT	CDSD	Warm dry UF	Dry UF
PSME/HODI	Douglas-fir/oceanspray	PA	CDS611	Warm moist UF	Moist UF
PSME/PHMA5	Douglas-fir/mallow ninebark	PA	CDS711	Warm dry UF	Dry UF
PSME/RIMO2/POPU3	Douglas-fir/mountain gooseberry/Jacob's ladder	PC	CDS911	Cold dry UF	Cold UF
PSME/SPBE2	Douglas-fir/birchleaf spiraea	PA	CDS634	Warm dry UF	Dry UF
PSME/SYAL	Douglas-fir/common snowberry	PA	CDS622	Warm dry UF	Dry UF
PSME/SYAL	Douglas-fir/common snowberry	PA	CDS624	Warm dry UF	Dry UF
PSME/SYAL (FLOODPLAIN)	Douglas-fir/common snowberry (floodplain)	PA	CDS628	Warm low SM RF	Low SM RF
PSME/SYOR2	Douglas-fir/mountain snowberry	PA	CDS623	Warm dry UF	Dry UF
PSME/SYOR2	Douglas-fir/mountain snowberry	PA	CDS625	Warm dry UF	Dry UF
PSME/SYOR2/CAGE2	Douglas-fir/mountain snowberry/elk sedge	PC	CDS642	Warm dry UF	Dry UF
PSME/TRCA	Douglas-fir/false bugbane	PCT	CDF313	Warm moderate SM RF	Warm RF

Table 8—Potential vegetation types (PVT) of the Blue Mountains section, organized by potential vegetation type code[a] (continued)

PVT code (PLANTS code)	PVT common name	Status	Ecoclass	PAG	PVG
PSME/VAME	Douglas-fir/big huckleberry	PA	CDS812	Warm dry UF	Dry UF
PSME/VAME	Douglas-fir/big huckleberry	PA	CDS821	Warm dry UF	Dry UF
PSME-PIPO-JUOC/FEID	Douglas-fir-ponderosa pine-western juniper/Idaho fescue	PC	CDG333	Warm dry UF	Dry UF
PTAQ-CAHO5	bracken fern-Hood's sedge	PC	FS8111	Cool moist UH	Cold UH
PUPA3	weak alkaligrass	PA	MM2926	Warm high SM RH	Warm RH
PUTR2/AGSP	bitterbrush/bluebunch wheatgrass	PA	SD3112	Hot moist US	Moist US
PUTR2/ERDO	bitterbrush/Douglas' buckwheat	PCT	SD3126	Warm dry US	Dry US
PUTR2/FEID-AGSP	bitterbrush/Idaho fescue-bluebunch wheatgrass	PA	SD3111	Warm moist US	Moist US
PUTR2-ARTRV/FEID	bitterbrush-mountain big sagebrush/Idaho fescue	PCT	SD3125	Warm moist US	Moist US
PUTR2-ARTRV/FEID-AGSP	bitterbrush-mountain big sagebrush/Idaho fescue-bluebunch wheatgrass	PA	SD3124	Warm moist US	Moist US
RHAL/MESIC FORB	alderleaf buckthorn/mesic forb	PCT	SW5117	Warm moderate SM RS	Warm RS
RHGL/AGSP	smooth sumac/bluebunch wheatgrass	PA	SD6121	Hot dry US	Dry US
RIBES/CILA2	currants/drooping woodreed	PCT	SW5111	Warm high SM RS	Warm RS
RIBES/GLEL	currants/tall mannagrass	PCT	SW5116	Warm high SM RS	Warm RS
RIBES/MESIC FORB	currants/mesic forb	PCT	SW5115	Warm moderate SM RS	Warm RS
ROCK OUTCROP	rock outcrop	PC	FS91	Cold dry UH	Cold UH
RUBA	Barton's raspberry	PC	SM5001	Hot low SM RS	Low SM RS
RUDI2	Himalayan blackberry	PC	SM5002	Hot moderate SM RS	Warm RS
RUOC2	western coneflower	PCT	FS8101	Warm moderate SM RH	Warm RH
RUOC2-MAGL2	western coneflower-cluster tarweed	PC	FS81	Cool moist UH	Cold UH
RUPA	thimbleberry	PCT	SM5912	Hot moderate SM RS	Warm RS
SAAR13	brook saxifrage	PCT	FW6113	Warm high SM RH	Warm RH
SAAR27	arctic willow	PA	SW1133	Cold high SM RS	Cold RS
SABO2/CASC12	Booth's willow/Holm's Rocky Mountain sedge	PA	SW1138	Cold high SM RS	Cold RS
SABO2/CAVE6	Booth's willow/inflated sedge	PC	SW1139	Cold high SM RS	Cold RS
SACO2/CAPR5	undergreen willow/clustered field sedge	PC	SW1128	Cold high SM RS	Cold RS
SACO2/CASC12	undergreen willow/Holm's Rocky Mountain sedge	PA	SW1121	Cold high SM RS	Cold RS
SACO2/CAUT	undergreen willow/bladder sedge	PCT	SW1127	Cold high SM RS	Cold RS
SADR/SETR	Drummond's willow/arrowleaf groundsel	PC	SW1137	Cold high SM RS	Cold RS
SAEA-SATW/CAAQ	Eastwood willow-Tweedy willow/aquatic sedge	PC	SW1129	Warm high SM RS	Warm RS
SAEX	coyote willow	PA	SW1117	Warm moderate SM RS	Warm RS
SAFA/ALVA	Farr's willow/Pacific onion	PC	SW1134	Cold high SM RS	Cold RS
SALE/MESIC FORB	Lemmon's willow/mesic forb	PCT	SW1135	Warm moderate SM RS	Warm RS
SALIX/CAAQ	willow/aquatic sedge	PA	SW1114	Cool high SM RS	Cold RS
SALIX/CACA4	willow/bluejoint reedgrass	PA	SW1124	Cool moderate SM RS	Cold RS
SALIX/CALA30	willow/woolly sedge	PA	SW1112	Warm moderate SM RS	Warm RS
SALIX/CAUT	willow/bladder sedge	PA	SW1123	Warm high SM RS	Warm RS
SALIX/MESIC FORB	willow/mesic forb	PCT	SW1125	Warm moderate SM RS	Warm RS
SALIX/POPR	willow/Kentucky bluegrass	PCT	SW1111	Warm low SM RS	Low SM RS
SARI2	rigid willow	PCT	SW1126	Hot moderate SM RS	Warm RS
SASC/ELGL	Scouler's willow/blue wildrye	PC	SW1130	Warm low SM RS	Low SM RS
SASI2/EQAR	Sitka willow/common horsetail	PC	SW1136	Warm high SM RS	Warm RS
SCMI2	smallfruit bulrush	PA	MM2924	Warm high SM RH	Warm RH
SCREE	scree	PC	FS90	Cold dry UH	Cold UH

Table 8—Potential vegetation types (PVT) of the Blue Mountains section, organized by potential vegetation type code[a] (continued)

PVT code (PLANTS code)	PVT common name	Status	Ecoclass	PAG	PVG
SETR	arrowleaf groundsel	PA	FW4211	Warm high SM RH	Warm RH
SETR-MILE2	arrowleaf groundsel-purple monkeyflower	PA	FW4214	Cool high SM RH	Cold RH
SPAN2	narrowleaf bur-reed	PA	WL0108	Cold high SM RH	Cold RH
SPCR (TERRACE)	sand dropseed (terrace)	PA	GB1211	Hot dry UH	Dry UH
STOC2	western needlegrass	PCT	GS10	Cool moist UH	Cold UH
STOC2-SIHY (ALPINE)	western needlegrass-squirreltail (alpine)	PCT	GS50	Warm dry UH	Dry UH
SYAL	common snowberry	PCT	SM31	Warm moist US	Moist US
SYAL (FLOODPLAIN)	common snowberry (floodplain)	PCT	SM33110	Hot moderate SM RS	Warm RS
SYAL/FEID-AGSP-LUSE4	common snowberry/Idaho fescue-bluebunch wheatgrass-silky lupine	PCT	GB5121	Warm moist US	Moist US
SYAL/FEID-KOCR	common snowberry/Idaho fescue-prairie junegrass	PCT	GB5919	Warm moist US	Moist US
SYAL-ROSA5	common snowberry-rose	PCT	SM31111	Warm moist US	Moist US
SYOR2	mountain snowberry	PCT	SM32	Warm moist US	Moist US
TSME/VAME	mountain hemlock/big huckleberry	PA	CMS231	Cold dry UF	Cold UF
TSME/VASC	mountain hemlock/grouse huckleberry	PA	CMS131	Cold dry UF	Cold UF
TURF	turf	PC	GS70	Cold dry UH	Cold UH
TYLA	common cattail	PC	MT8121	Hot high SM RH	Warm RH
VEAM2	American speedwell	PA	FW6112	Warm high SM RH	Warm RH
VERAT	false hellebore	PCT	FW51	Warm moderate SM RH	Warm RH
VERAT	false hellebore	PC	FW5121	Warm moderate SM RH	Warm RH

[a] This tabular summary is organized alphabetically by PVT code (USDA Forest Service 2002). Column descriptions are:

"PVT code" provides an alphanumeric code for each potential vegetation type; see "naming conventions" section for information about derivation of PVT codes. Note that a PVT code might be listed twice, in which case the same potential vegetation type was included in more than one potential vegetation classification for the Blue Mountains section (Crowe and Clausnitzer 1997, Johnson 2004, Johnson and Clausnitzer 1992, Johnson and Simon 1987, Johnson and Swanson 2005, Wells 2006), but a different ecoclass code was assigned for each instance. PLANTS code (USDA NRCS 2004) is described in the species list section of this report.

"PVT common name" provides a common name for each potential vegetation type; see "naming conventions" section for information about derivation of PVT common names.

"Status" provides the classification status of each potential vegetation type: PA is plant association; PC is plant community; PCT is plant community type.

"Ecoclass" codes are used to record potential vegetation type determinations on field forms and in computer databases; see "naming conventions" section for information about derivation of ecoclass codes.

"PAG" (plant association group) and "PVG" (potential vegetation group) are two of the midscale hierarchical units (fig. 2); PAG and PVG codes use the following abbreviations: SM is soil moisture, UF is upland forest physiognomic class, UW is upland woodland physiognomic class, US is upland shrub physiognomic class, UH is upland herb physiognomic class, RF is riparian forest physiognomic class, RS is riparian shrub physiognomic class, and RH is riparian herb physiognomic class.

Table 9—Potential vegetation types (PVT) of the Blue Mountains section, organized by ecoclass code[a]

Ecoclass	PVT code (PLANTS code)	PVT common name	Status	PAG	PVG
CAF0	ABLA-PIAL/POPU3	subalpine fir-whitebark pine/Jacob's ladder	PC	Cold dry UF	Cold UF
CAF2	ABLA-PIAL/POPH	subalpine fir-whitebark pine/alpine fleeceflower	PCT	Cold dry UF	Cold UF
CAF322	PIAL/ARAC2	whitebark pine/prickly sandwort	PCT	Cold dry UF	Cold UF
CAF323	PIAL/LUAR3	whitebark pine/silvery lupine	PC	Cold dry UF	Cold UF
CAF324	ABLA-PIAL/ARAC2	subalpine fir-whitebark pine/prickly sandwort	PC	Cold dry UF	Cold UF
CAG111	ABLA/CAGE2	subalpine fir/elk sedge	PA	Cold dry UF	Cold UF
CAG131	PIAL/CAGE2	whitebark pine/elk sedge	PA	Cold dry UF	Cold UF
CAG132	ABLA-PIAL/JUPA-STLE2	subalpine fir-whitebark pine/Parry's rush-Lemmon's needlegrass	PA	Cold dry UF	Cold UF
CAG133	ABLA-PIAL/CAGE2	subalpine fir-whitebark pine/elk sedge	PA	Cold dry UF	Cold UF
CAG221	PIAL/FEVI	whitebark pine/green fescue	PA	Cold dry UF	Cold UF
CAG222	ABLA-PIAL/FEVI	subalpine fir-whitebark pine/green fescue	PA	Cold dry UF	Cold UF
CAG3	ABLA-PIAL/JUDR	subalpine fir-whitebark pine/Drummond's rush	PCT	Cold dry UF	Cold UF
CAS311	PIAL/VASC/LUHI4	whitebark pine/grouse huckleberry/smooth woodrush	PA	Cold dry UF	Cold UF
CAS312	PIAL/VASC/ARCO9	whitebark pine/grouse huckleberry/heartleaf arnica	PC	Cold dry UF	Cold UF
CAS313	PIAL/VASC/ARAC2	whitebark pine/grouse huckleberry/prickly sandwort	PC	Cold dry UF	Cold UF
CAS422	PIAL/JUCO6-ARNE	whitebark pine/mountain juniper-pinemat manzanita	PC	Cold dry UF	Cold UF
CAS423	ABLA-PIAL/JUCO6-ARNE	subalpine fir-whitebark pine/mountain juniper-pinemat manzanita	PC	Cold dry UF	Cold UF
CAS424	ABLA-PIAL/JUCO6	subalpine fir-whitebark pine/mountain juniper	PC	Cold dry UF	Cold UF
CAS511	PIFL2/JUCO6	limber pine/mountain juniper	PA	Cold dry UF	Cold UF
CAS512	PIAL/RIMO2/POPU3	whitebark pine/mountain gooseberry/Jacob's ladder	PA	Cold dry UF	Cold UF
CAS611	ABLA-PIAL/RIMO2/POPU3	subalpine fir-whitebark pine/mountain gooseberry/Jacob's ladder	PCT	Cold dry UF	Cold UF
CAS621	ABLA-PIAL/VASC/ARCO9	subalpine fir-whitebark pine/grouse huckleberry/heartleaf arnica	PA	Cold dry UF	Cold UF
CAS622	ABLA-PIAL/VASC/CARO5	subalpine fir-whitebark pine/grouse huckleberry/Ross' sedge	PA	Cold dry UF	Cold UF
CAS623	ABLA-PIAL/VASC/ARAC2	subalpine fir-whitebark pine/grouse huckleberry/prickly sandwort	PCT	Cold dry UF	Cold UF
CAS624	ABLA-PIAL/VASC-PHEM	subalpine fir-whitebark pine/grouse huckleberry-pink mountainheath	PCT	Cold dry UF	Cold UF
CAS625	ABLA-PIAL/VASC/FEVI	subalpine fir-whitebark pine/grouse huckleberry/green fescue	PC	Cold dry UF	Cold UF
CAS626	ABLA-PIAL/VASC/OREX	subalpine fir-whitebark pine/grouse huckleberry/little ricegrass	PC	Cold dry UF	Cold UF
CAS627	ABLA-PIAL/VASC/LECOW2	subalpine fir-whitebark pine/grouse huckleberry/Wallowa Lewisia	PC	Cold dry UF	Cold UF
CAS628	ABLA-PIAL/VASC-PHEM (AVALANCHE)	subalpine fir-whitebark pine/grouse huckleberry-pink mountainheath (avalanche)	PC	Cold dry UF	Cold UF
CAS629	ABLA-PIAL/VASC/FEVI (AVALANCHE)	subalpine fir-whitebark pine/grouse huckleberry/green fescue (avalanche)	PC	Cold dry UF	Cold UF
CDF313	PSME/TRCA	Douglas-fir/false bugbane	PCT	Warm moderate SM RF	Warm RF
CDG111	PSME/CAGE2	Douglas-fir/elk sedge	PA	Warm dry UF	Dry UF
CDG112	PSME/CARU	Douglas-fir/pinegrass	PA	Warm dry UF	Dry UF
CDG121	PSME/CARU	Douglas-fir/pinegrass	PA	Warm dry UF	Dry UF
CDG333	PSME-PIPO-JUOC/FEID	Douglas-fir-ponderosa pine-western juniper/Idaho fescue	PC	Warm dry UF	Dry UF
CDS611	PSME/HODI	Douglas-fir/oceanspray	PA	Warm moist UF	Moist UF
CDS622	PSME/SYAL	Douglas-fir/common snowberry	PA	Warm dry UF	Dry UF
CDS623	PSME/SYOR2	Douglas-fir/mountain snowberry	PA	Warm dry UF	Dry UF
CDS624	PSME/SYAL	Douglas-fir/common snowberry	PA	Warm dry UF	Dry UF

Table 9—Potential vegetation types (PVT) of the Blue Mountains section, organized by ecoclass code[a] (continued)

Ecoclass	PVT code (PLANTS code)	PVT common name	Status	PAG	PVG
CDS625	PSME/SYOR2	Douglas-fir/mountain snowberry	PA	Warm dry UF	Dry UF
CDS628	PSME/SYAL (FLOODPLAIN)	Douglas-fir/common snowberry (floodplain)	PA	Warm low SM RF	Low SM RF
CDS634	PSME/SPBE2	Douglas-fir/birchleaf spiraea	PA	Warm dry UF	Dry UF
CDS642	PSME/SYOR2/CAGE2	Douglas-fir/mountain snowberry/elk sedge	PC	Warm dry UF	Dry UF
CDS664	PSME/ARNE/CAGE2	Douglas-fir/pinemat manzanita/elk sedge	PA	Warm dry UF	Dry UF
CDS711	PSME/PHMA5	Douglas-fir/mallow ninebark	PA	Warm dry UF	Dry UF
CDS722	PSME/ACGL-PHMA5	Douglas-fir/Rocky Mountain maple-mallow ninebark	PA	Warm moist UF	Moist UF
CDS724	PSME/ACGL-PHMA5 (FLOODPLAIN)	Douglas-fir/Rocky Mountain maple-mallow ninebark (floodplain)	PA	Warm moderate SM RF	Warm RF
CDS725	PSME/ACGL-SYOR2	Douglas-fir/Rocky Mountain maple-mountain snowberry	PC	Warm moist UF	Moist UF
CDS812	PSME/VAME	Douglas-fir/big huckleberry	PA	Warm dry UF	Dry UF
CDS821	PSME/VAME	Douglas-fir/big huckleberry	PA	Warm dry UF	Dry UF
CDS911	PSME/RIMO2/POPU3	Douglas-fir/mountain gooseberry/Jacob's ladder	PC	Cold dry UF	Cold UF
CDSD	PSME/CELE3/CAGE2	Douglas-fir/mountain mahogany/elk sedge	PCT	Warm dry UF	Dry UF
CEF111	ABLA/XETE	subalpine fir/beargrass	PA	Cool dry UF	Cold UF
CEF2	ABLA-PIEN/LIBO3	subalpine fir-Engelmann spruce/twinflower	PC	Cool moist UF	Moist UF
CEF221	ABLA/LIBO3	subalpine fir/twinflower	PA	Cool moist UF	Moist UF
CEF311	ABLA/STAM2	subalpine fir/claspleaf twistedstalk	PCT	Cool wet UF	Moist UF
CEF331	ABLA/TRCA	subalpine fir/false bugbane	PA	Cool moist UF	Moist UF
CEF332	ABLA/ATFI	subalpine fir/ladyfern	PA	Cold high SM RF	Cold RF
CEF333	ABLA/SETR	subalpine fir/arrowleaf groundsel	PA	Cold high SM RF	Cold RF
CEF334	PIEN/ATFI	Engelmann spruce/ladyfern	PCT	Cold high SM RF	Cold RF
CEF335	PIEN/SETR	Engelmann spruce/arrowleaf groundsel	PA	Cold high SM RF	Cold RF
CEF336	ABLA-PIEN/SETR	subalpine fir-Engelmann spruce/arrowleaf groundsel	PC	Cold moist UF	Cold UF
CEF411	ABLA/POPU3	subalpine fir/Jacob's ladder	PA	Cold dry UF	Cold UF
CEF412	ABLA/ARCO9	subalpine fir/heartleaf arnica	PCT	Cool moist UF	Moist UF
CEF425	ABLA-PIEN/TRCA	subalpine fir-Engelmann spruce/false bugbane	PC	Cool moist UF	Moist UF
CEF426	ABLA-PIEN/POPU3	subalpine fir-Engelmann spruce/Jacob's ladder	PC	Cold dry UF	Cold UF
CEF435	ABLA/ARCO9	subalpine fir/heartleaf arnica	PA	Cool moist UF	Moist UF
CEF436	ABLA-PIEN/ARCO9	subalpine fir-Engelmann spruce/heartleaf arnica	PA	Cool moist UF	Moist UF
CEF437	ABLA-PIEN/CLUN2	subalpine fir-Engelmann spruce/queencup beadlily	PA	Cool moist UF	Moist UF
CEF511	ABLA/POPH	subalpine fir/alpine fleeceflower	PC	Cold dry UF	Cold UF
CEG131	ABLA-PIEN/LUHI4	subalpine fir-Engelmann spruce/smooth woodrush	PC	Cold dry UF	Cold UF
CEG201	PIEN-ABLA/CASC12	Engelmann spruce-subalpine fir/Holm's Rocky Mountain sedge	PA	Cold high SM RF	Cold RF
CEG312	ABLA/CARU	subalpine fir/pinegrass	PA	Cool dry UF	Cold UF
CEG323	ABLA/STOC2	subalpine fir/western needlegrass	PCT	Cold dry UF	Cold UF
CEG411	ABLA/FEVI	subalpine fir/green fescue	PC	Cold dry UF	Cold UF
CEG412	ABLA/JUDR	subalpine fir/Drummond's rush	PC	Cold dry UF	Cold UF
CEG413	ABLA/JUTE	subalpine fir/slender rush	PC	Cold dry UF	Cold UF
CEG414	ABLA/JUPA (AVALANCHE)	subalpine fir/Parry's rush (avalanche)	PC	Cold dry UF	Cold UF
CEM121	PIEN/CADI6	Engelmann spruce/softleaf sedge	PA	Cold high SM RF	Cold RF
CEM122	ABLA/CADI6	subalpine fir/softleaf sedge	PCT	Cold high SM RF	Cold RF
CEM123	ABLA/CAAQ	subalpine fir/aquatic sedge	PCT	Cold high SM RF	Cold RF
CEM124	ABLA/CACA4	subalpine fir/bluejoint reedgrass	PA	Cold moderate SM RF	Cold RF
CEM125	PIEN/BRVU	Engelmann spruce/Columbia brome	PCT	Cold low SM RF	Cold RF

77

Table 9—Potential vegetation types (PVT) of the Blue Mountains section, organized by ecoclass code[a] (continued)

Ecoclass	PVT code (PLANTS code)	PVT common name	Status	PAG	PVG
CEM126	PIEN/CILA2	Engelmann spruce/drooping woodreed	PC	Cold moderate SM RF	Cold RF
CEM201	PIEN-ABLA/SETR	Engelmann spruce-subalpine fir/arrowleaf groundsel	PA	Cold high SM RF	Cold RF
CEM211	PIEN/EQAR	Engelmann spruce/common horsetail	PA	Cold moderate SM RF	Cold RF
CES313	ABLA/VAUL/CASC12	subalpine fir/bog blueberry/Holm's Rocky Mountain sedge	PCT	Cold high SM RF	Cold RF
CES131	ABLA/CLUN2	subalpine fir/queencup beadlily	PA	Cold moist UF	Moist UF
CES2	ABLA-PIEN/MEFE	subalpine fir-Engelmann spruce/rusty menziesia	PA	Cold moist UF	Cold UF
CES214	ABLA/RHAL2	subalpine fir/white rhododendron	PCT	Cold moist UF	Cold UF
CES215	ABLA-PIEN/RHAL2	subalpine fir-Engelmann spruce/white rhododendron	PC	Cold moist UF	Cold UF
CES221	ABLA/MEFE	subalpine fir/rusty menziesia	PA	Cold moist UF	Cold UF
CES311	ABLA/VAME	subalpine fir/big huckleberry	PA	Cool moist UF	Moist UF
CES314	ABLA/CLUN2	subalpine fir/queencup beadlily	PA	Cool moist UF	Moist UF
CES315	ABLA/VAME	subalpine fir/big huckleberry	PA	Cool moist UF	Moist UF
CES316	ABLA/VAME (FLOODPLAIN)	subalpine fir/big huckleberry (floodplain)	PA	Cold moderate SM RF	Cold RF
CES411	ABLA/VASC	subalpine fir/grouse huckleberry	PA	Cold dry UF	Moist UF
CES414	ABLA/LIBO3	subalpine fir/twinflower	PA	Cool moist UF	Cold UF
CES415	ABLA/VASC/POPU3	subalpine fir/grouse huckleberry/Jacob's ladder	PA	Cold dry UF	Cold UF
CES427	ABLA-PIEN/VASC-PHEM	subalpine fir-Engelmann spruce/grouse huckleberry-pink mountainheath	PC	Cold dry UF	Cold UF
CES428	ABLA/VASC-PHEM	subalpine fir/grouse huckleberry-pink mountainheath	PA	Cold dry UF	Cold UF
CES429	ABLA/ARNE/ARAC2	subalpine fir/pinemat manzanita/prickly sandwort	PC	Cool dry UF	Cold UF
CES511	PIEN/COST4	Engelmann spruce/red osier dogwood	PA	Cold moderate SM RF	Cold RF
CES610	ABLA-PIEN/LEGL (FLOODPLAIN)	subalpine fir-Engelmann spruce/Labrador tea (floodplain)	PA	Cold high SM RF	Cold RF
CES612	ABLA-PIEN/LEGL	subalpine fir-Engelmann spruce/Labrador tea	PA	Cold moist UF	Cold UF
CES710	ABLA-PIEN/MEFE (FLOODPLAIN)	subalpine fir-Engelmann spruce/rusty menziesia (floodplain)	PA	Cold moderate SM RF	Cold RF
CES8	ABLA-PIMO3/CHUM	subalpine fir-western white pine/prince's pine	PC	Cool dry UF	Cold UF
CJC1	JUCO6	mountain juniper	PC	Warm moist US	Moist US
CJG111	JUOC/FEID-AGSP	western juniper/Idaho fescue-bluebunch wheatgrass	PA	Hot moist UW	Moist UW
CJG113	JUOC/AGSP	western juniper/bluebunch wheatgrass	PCT	Hot dry UW	Dry UW
CJS1	JUOC/ARAR8	western juniper/low sagebrush	PCT	Hot dry UW	Dry UW
CJS112	JUOC/ARAR8/FEID	western juniper/low sagebrush/Idaho fescue	PA	Hot dry UW	Dry UW
CJS2	JUOC/ARTRV/FEID-AGSP	western juniper/mountain big sagebrush/Idaho fescue-bluebunch wheatgrass	PCT	Hot moist UW	Moist UW
CJS321	JUOC/PUTR2/FEID-AGSP	western juniper/bitterbrush/Idaho fescue-bluebunch wheatgrass	PA	Hot moist UW	Moist UW
CJS41	JUOC/CELE3/FEID-AGSP	western juniper/mountain mahogany/Idaho fescue-bluebunch wheatgrass	PA	Hot moist UW	Moist UW
CJS42	JUOC/CELE3/CAGE2	western juniper/mountain mahogany/elk sedge	PCT	Hot moist UW	Moist UW
CJS5	JUSC2/CELE3	Rocky Mountain juniper-mountain mahogany	PC	Warm dry UF	Dry UF
CJS8	JUOC/ARRI2	western juniper/stiff sagebrush	PCT	Hot dry UW	Dry UW
CJS811	JUOC/ARRI2 (SCAB)	western juniper/stiff sagebrush (scabland)	PCT	Hot dry UW	Dry UW
CLF211	PICO(ABGR)/LIBO3	lodgepole pine(grand fir)/twinflower	PCT	Cool moist UF	Moist UF
CLG11	PICO(ABLA)/STOC2	lodgepole pine(subalpine fir)/western needlegrass	PCT	Cold dry UF	Cold UF
CLG21	PICO(ABGR)/CARU	lodgepole pine(grand fir)/pinegrass	PCT	Cool dry UF	Cold UF
CLG322	PICO(ABLA)/CAGE2	lodgepole pine(subalpine fir)/elk sedge	PCT	Cold dry UF	Cold UF
CLM112	PICO/POPR	lodgepole pine/Kentucky bluegrass	PCT	Cold low SM RF	Cold RF
CLM114	PICO/CAAQ	lodgepole pine/aquatic sedge	PA	Cold high SM RF	Cold RF
CLM115	PICO/DECE	lodgepole pine/tufted hairgrass	PA	Cold moderate SM RF	Cold RF
CLM116	PICO/CALA30	lodgepole pine/woolly sedge	PC	Cold moderate SM RF	Cold RF

Table 9—Potential vegetation types (PVT) of the Blue Mountains section, organized by ecoclass code[a] (continued)

Ecoclass	PVT code (PLANTS code)	PVT common name	Status	PAG	PVG
CLM117	PICO/CACA4	lodgepole pine/bluejoint reedgrass	PC	Cold moderate SM RF	Cold RF
CLM118	PICO/CASC12	lodgepole pine/Holm's Rocky Mountain sedge	PC	Cold high SM RF	Cold RF
CLM511	PICO/ALIN2/MESIC FORB	lodgepole pine/mountain alder/mesic forb	PC	Cold moderate SM RF	Cold RF
CLS415	PICO(ABLA)/VASC/POPU3	lodgepole pine(subalpine fir)/grouse huckleberry/Jacob's ladder	PCT	Cold dry UF	Cold UF
CLS416	PICO/CARU	lodgepole pine/pinegrass	PA	Cool dry UF	Cold UF
CLS417	PICO(ABGR)/VASC/CARU	lodgepole pine(grand fir)/grouse huckleberry/pinegrass	PCT	Cold dry UF	Cold UF
CLS418	PICO(ABLA)/VASC	lodgepole pine(subalpine fir)/grouse huckleberry	PCT	Cold dry UF	Cold UF
CLS5	PICO(ABGR)/VAME-LIBO3	lodgepole pine(grand fir)/big huckleberry/twinflower	PCT	Cool moist UF	Moist UF
CLS512	PICO(ABGR)/VAME/CARU	lodgepole pine(grand fir)/big huckleberry/pinegrass	PCT	Cool moist UF	Moist UF
CLS513	PICO(ABGR)/VAME	lodgepole pine(grand fir)/big huckleberry	PCT	Cool moist UF	Moist UF
CLS514	PICO(ABLA)/VAME	lodgepole pine(subalpine fir)/big huckleberry	PCT	Cool moist UF	Moist UF
CLS515	PICO(ABLA)/VAME	lodgepole pine(subalpine fir)/big huckleberry	PCT	Cool moist UF	Moist UF
CLS516	PICO(ABLA)/VAME/CARU	lodgepole pine(subalpine fir)/big huckleberry/pinegrass	PCT	Cool moist UF	Moist UF
CLS519	PICO(ABGR)/VAME/PTAQ	lodgepole pine(grand fir)/big huckleberry/bracken fern	PCT	Cool moist UF	Moist UF
CLS57	PICO(ABGR)/ARNE	lodgepole pine(grand fir)/pinemat manzanita	PCT	Cool dry UF	Cold UF
CLS58	PICO(ABGR)/ALSI3	lodgepole pine(grand fir)/Sitka alder	PCT	Cool very moist UF	Moist UF
CMS131	TSME/VASC	mountain hemlock/grouse huckleberry	PA	Cold dry UF	Cold UF
CMS231	TSME/VAME	mountain hemlock/big huckleberry	PA	Cold dry UF	Cold UF
CPC212	PIPO-JUOC/CELE3-SYOR2	ponderosa pine-western juniper/mountain mahogany-mountain snowberry	PCT	Hot dry UF	Dry UF
CPG111	PIPO/AGSP	ponderosa pine/bluebunch wheatgrass	PA	Hot dry UF	Dry UF
CPG112	PIPO/FEID	ponderosa pine/Idaho fescue	PA	Hot dry UF	Dry UF
CPG131	PIPO/FEID	ponderosa pine/Idaho fescue	PA	Hot dry UF	Dry UF
CPG132	PIPO/AGSP	ponderosa pine/bluebunch wheatgrass	PA	Hot dry UF	Dry UF
CPG221	PIPO/CARU	ponderosa pine/pinegrass	PA	Warm dry UF	Dry UF
CPG222	PIPO/CAGE2	ponderosa pine/elk sedge	PA	Warm dry UF	Dry UF
CPM112	PIPO/POPR	ponderosa pine/Kentucky bluegrass	PCT	Hot low SM RF	Low SM RF
CPS131	PIPO/ARTRV/FEID-AGSP	ponderosa pine/mountain big sagebrush/Idaho fescue-bluebunch wheatgrass	PA	Hot dry UF	Dry UF
CPS132	PIPO/ARTRV/CAGE2	ponderosa pine/mountain big sagebrush/elk sedge	PCT	Hot dry UF	Dry UF
CPS221	PIPO/PUTR2/CARO5	ponderosa pine/bitterbrush/Ross' sedge	PA	Warm dry UF	Dry UF
CPS222	PIPO/PUTR2/CAGE2	ponderosa pine/bitterbrush/elk sedge	PA	Warm dry UF	Dry UF
CPS226	PIPO/PUTR2/FEID-AGSP	ponderosa pine/bitterbrush/Idaho fescue-bluebunch wheatgrass	PA	Hot dry UF	Dry UF
CPS229	PIPO/PUTR2/AGSP-POSA12	ponderosa pine/bitterbrush/bluebunch wheatgrass-Sandberg's bluegrass	PA	Hot dry UF	Dry UF
CPS231	PIPO/PUTR2/AGSP	ponderosa pine/bitterbrush/bluebunch wheatgrass	PCT	Hot dry UF	Dry UF
CPS232	PIPO/CELE3/CAGE2	ponderosa pine/mountain mahogany/elk sedge	PA	Warm dry UF	Dry UF
CPS233	PIPO/CELE3/PONEW	ponderosa pine/mountain mahogany/Wheeler's bluegrass	PA	Hot dry UF	Dry UF
CPS234	PIPO/CELE3/FEID-AGSP	ponderosa pine/mountain mahogany/Idaho fescue-bluebunch wheatgrass	PA	Hot dry UF	Dry UF
CPS511	PIPO/SYAL (FLOODPLAIN)	ponderosa pine/common snowberry (floodplain)	PA	Hot low SM RF	Low SM RF
CPS522	PIPO/SYAL	ponderosa pine/common snowberry	PA	Warm dry UF	Dry UF
CPS523	PIPO/SPBE2	ponderosa pine/birchleaf spiraea	PCT	Warm dry UF	Dry UF
CPS524	PIPO/SYAL	ponderosa pine/common snowberry	PA	Warm dry UF	Dry UF
CPS525	PIPO/SYOR2	ponderosa pine/mountain snowberry	PA	Warm dry UF	Dry UF
CPS61	PIPO/ARAR8	ponderosa pine/low sagebrush	PCT	Hot moist UF	Dry UF
CPS722	PIPO/CRDO2	ponderosa pine/black hawthorn	PC	Hot moderate SM RF	Warm RF
CPS8	PIPO/PERA4	ponderosa pine/squaw apple	PCT	Hot dry UF	Dry UF

Table 9—Potential vegetation types (PVT) of the Blue Mountains section, organized by ecoclass code[a] (continued)

Ecoclass	PVT code (PLANTS code)	PVT common name	Status	PAG	PVG
CPS9	PIPO/RHGL	ponderosa pine/smooth sumac	PCT	Hot dry UF	Dry UF
CQM111	PIMO3/DECE	western white pine/tufted hairgrass	PCT	Warm moderate SM RF	Warm RF
CWC811	ABGR/TABR2/CLUN2	grand fir/Pacific yew/queencup beadlily	PA	Cool wet UF	Moist UF
CWC812	ABGR/TABR2/LIBO3	grand fir/Pacific yew/twinflower	PA	Cool wet UF	Moist UF
CWF311	ABGR/LIBO3	grand fir/twinflower	PA	Cool moist UF	Moist UF
CWF312	ABGR/LIBO3	grand fir/twinflower	PA	Cool moist UF	Moist UF
CWF421	ABGR/CLUN2	grand fir/queencup beadlily	PA	Cool moist UF	Moist UF
CWF422	ABGR/TABR2/CLUN2	grand fir/Pacific yew/queencup beadlily	PA	Cool moist UF	Moist UF
CWF424	ABGR/TABR2/LIBO3 (FLOODPLAIN)	grand fir/Pacific yew/twinflower (floodplain)	PA	Cool wet UF	Warm RF
CWF444	ABGR/ARCO9	grand fir/heartleaf arnica	PCT	Cold dry UF	Cold UF
CWF511	ABGR/COOC	grand fir/goldthread	PA	Cool dry UF	Cold UF
CWF512	ABGR/TRCA	grand fir/false bugbane	PA	Cool very moist UF	Moist UF
CWF611	ABGR/GYDR	grand fir/oakfern	PA	Cool very moist UF	Moist UF
CWF612	ABGR/POMU-ASCA2	grand fir/swordfern-ginger	PA	Cool very moist UF	Moist UF
CWF613	ABGR/ATFI	grand fir/ladyfern	PA	Warm high SM RF	Warm RF
CWG111	ABGR/CAGE2	grand fir/elk sedge	PA	Warm dry UF	Dry UF
CWG112	ABGR/CARU	grand fir/pinegrass	PA	Warm dry UF	Dry UF
CWG113	ABGR/CARU	grand fir/pinegrass	PA	Warm dry UF	Dry UF
CWG211	ABGR/BRVU	grand fir/Columbia brome	PA	Warm moist UF	Moist UF
CWM311	ABGR/CALA30	grand fir/woolly sedge	PC	Warm high SM RF	Warm RF
CWS211	ABGR/VAME	grand fir/big huckleberry	PA	Cool moist UF	Moist UF
CWS212	ABGR/VAME	grand fir/big huckleberry	PA	Cool moist UF	Moist UF
CWS232	ABGR-CHNO/VAME	grand fir-Alaska yellow cedar/big huckleberry	PCT	Cool moist UF	Moist UF
CWS314	ABGR/SYAL (FLOODPLAIN)	grand fir/common snowberry (floodplain)	PCT	Warm low SM RF	Low SM RF
CWS321	ABGR/SPBE2	grand fir/birchleaf spiraea	PA	Warm dry UF	Dry UF
CWS322	ABGR/SPBE2	grand fir/birchleaf spiraea	PA	Warm dry UF	Dry UF
CWS412	ABGR/ACGL-PHMA5	grand fir/Rocky Mountain maple-mallow ninebark	PCT	Warm moist UF	Moist UF
CWS423	ABGR/CRDO2/CADE9	grand fir/black hawthorn/Dewey's sedge	PA	Warm high SM RF	Warm RF
CWS541	ABGR/ACGL	grand fir/Rocky Mountain maple	PA	Warm very moist UF	Moist UF
CWS543	ABGR/ACGL (FLOODPLAIN)	grand fir/Rocky Mountain maple (floodplain)	PA	Warm moderate SM RF	Warm RF
CWS811	ABGR/VASC	grand fir/grouse huckleberry	PA	Cold dry UF	Cold UF
CWS812	ABGR/VASC-LIBO3	grand fir/grouse huckleberry-twinflower	PA	Cool moist UF	Moist UF
CWS912	ABGR/ACGL	grand fir/Rocky Mountain maple	PA	Warm very moist UF	Moist UF
FM9111	ERDO-POSA12	Douglas' buckwheat-Sandberg's bluegrass	PCT	Hot dry UH	Dry UH
FM9112	ERST4-POSA12	strict buckwheat/Sandberg's bluegrass	PCT	Hot dry UH	Dry UH
FM9113	ERUM (RIDGE)	sulphurflower (ridge)	PCT	Hot dry UH	Dry UH
FS1113	LINU4-CYTEF	linanthus-cymopterus	PC	Cool dry UH	Cold UH
FS5912	POPH-FEVI	alpine fleeceflower-green fescue	PC	Cold moist UH	Cold moist UH
FS5913	POPH-CARU-CAGE2	alpine fleeceflower-pinegrass-elk sedge	PC	Cool dry UH	Cold UH
FS5914	POPH-CAGE2-LINU4	alpine fleeceflower-elk sedge-linanthus	PC	Cool dry UH	Cold UH
FS5915	POPH-AGUR-LINU4	alpine fleeceflower-horsemint-linanthus	PC	Cool dry UH	Cold UH
FS5916	POPH (CORNICES)	alpine fleeceflower (cornices)	PC	Cold moist UH	Cold moist UH
FS80	LINU4-ARLU	linanthus-white sagebrush	PC	Cool dry UH	Cold UH
FS81	RUOC2-MAGL2	western coneflower-cluster tarweed	PC	Cool moist UH	Cold UH

Table 9—Potential vegetation types (PVT) of the Blue Mountains section, organized by ecoclass code[a] (continued)

Ecoclass	PVT code (PLANTS code)	PVT common name	Status	PAG	PVG
FS8101	RUOC2	western coneflower	PCT	Warm moderate SM RH	Warm RH
FS8111	PTAQ-CAHO5	bracken fern-Hood's sedge	PC	Cool dry UH	Cold UH
FS8112	MOOD	mountain balm	PC	Cool dry UH	Cold UH
FS8113	LEPY2-MAGL2	pygmy Lewisia-cluster tarweed	PC	Cool moist UH	Cold UH
FS8115	LINU4-ARLO6	linanthus-longleaf arnica	PC	Cool moist UH	Cold UH
FS8116	ERFL4-PECO	golden buckwheat-coiled lousewort	PC	Cool dry UH	Cold UH
FS8117	PHLOX-CYTEF	phlox-cymopteris	PC	Cold dry UH	Cold UH
FS8118	PHLOX-IVGO	phlox-Ivesia	PC	Cold dry UH	Cold UH
FS90	SCREE	scree	PC	Cold dry UH	Cold UH
FS91	ROCK OUTCROP	rock outcrop	PC	Cold dry UH	Cold UH
FS92	GRUS	grus	PC	Cold dry UH	Cold UH
FW3911	CACU2 (SEEP)	Cusick's camas (seep)	PCT	Warm very moist UH	Moist UH
FW4211	SETR	arrowleaf groundsel	PA	Warm high SM RH	Warm RH
FW4212	EQAR	common horsetail	PA	Warm moderate SM RH	Warm RH
FW4213	ADPE	maidenhair fern	PCT	Warm high SM RH	Warm RH
FW4214	SETR-MILE2	arrowleaf groundsel-purple monkeyflower	PA	Cool high SM RH	Cold RH
FW51	VERAT	false hellebore	PCT	Warm moderate SM RH	Warm RH
FW5121	VERAT	false hellebore	PC	Warm moderate SM RH	Warm RH
FW6111	METR3	buckbean	PC	Warm high SM RH	Warm RH
FW6112	VEAM2	American speedwell	PA	Warm high SM RH	Warm RH
FW6113	SAAR13	brook saxifrage	PCT	Warm high SM RH	Warm RH
[none]	ALVA	Pacific onion	PCT	Cold high SM RH	Cold RH
FW7111	ALVA-CASC12	Pacific onion-Holm's Rocky Mountain sedge	PA	Cold high SM RH	Cold RH
FX4111	LECOW2 (RIM)	Wallowa Lewisia (rim)	PCT	Hot dry UH	Dry UH
GB1221	SPCR (TERRACE)	sand dropseed (terrace)	PA	Hot dry UH	Dry UH
GB1911	AGSP-SPCR-ARLO3	bluebunch wheatgrass-sand dropseed-red threeawn	PCT	Hot dry UH	Dry UH
GB41	AGSP-POSA12	bluebunch wheatgrass-Sandberg's bluegrass	PA	Hot dry UH	Dry UH
GB4111	AGSP-ERHE2	bluebunch wheatgrass-Wyeth's buckwheat	PA	Hot dry UH	Dry UH
GB4112	AGSP-POSA12-SCAN3	bluebunch wheatgrass-Sandberg's bluegrass-narrowleaf skullcap	PA	Hot dry UH	Dry UH
GB4113	AGSP-POSA12 (BASALT)	bluebunch wheatgrass-Sandberg's bluegrass (basalt)	PA	Hot dry UH	Dry UH
GB4114	AGSP-POSA12-ASCU5	bluebunch wheatgrass-Sandberg's bluegrass-Cusick's milkvetch	PA	Hot dry UH	Dry UH
GB4115	AGSP-POSA12-ERPU2	bluebunch wheatgrass-Sandberg's bluegrass-shaggy fleabane	PA	Hot dry UH	Dry UH
GB4116	AGSP-POSA12 (GRANITE)	bluebunch wheatgrass-Sandberg's bluegrass (granite)	PA	Hot dry UH	Dry UH
GB4117	AGSP-POSA12-PHCO10	bluebunch wheatgrass-Sandberg's bluegrass-Snake River phlox	PA	Hot dry UH	Dry UH
GB4118	AGSP-POSA12-OPPO	bluebunch wheatgrass-Sandberg's bluegrass-pricklypear	PA	Hot dry UH	Dry UH
GB4119	AGSP-POSA12-LUPIN	bluebunch wheatgrass-Sandberg's bluegrass-lupine	PA	Hot dry UH	Dry UH
GB4121	AGSP-POSA12	bluebunch wheatgrass-Sandberg's bluegrass	PA	Hot dry UH	Dry UH
GB4123	AGSP-POSA12-BASA3	bluebunch wheatgrass-Sandberg's bluegrass-arrowleaf balsamroot	PA	Hot dry UH	Dry UH
GB4124	AGSP-POSA12-ERHE2	bluebunch wheatgrass-Sandberg's bluegrass-creamy buckwheat	PA	Hot dry UH	Dry UH
GB4125	AGSP-POSA12-ASRE5	bluebunch wheatgrass-Sandberg's bluegrass-Blue Mountain milkvetch	PA	Hot dry UH	Dry UH
GB4126	AGSP-POSA12-TRMA3	bluebunch wheatgrass-Sandberg's bluegrass-bighead clover	PA	Hot dry UH	Dry UH
GB4127	AGSP-POSA12-APAN2	bluebunch wheatgrass-Sandberg's bluegrass-spreading dogbane	PA	Hot dry UH	Dry UH
GB4131	AGSP-BRCA5	bluebunch wheatgrass-mountain brome	PCT	Warm moist UH	Moist UH
GB4132	AGSP-ERUM	bluebunch wheatgrass-sulphurflower buckwheat	PCT	Hot dry UH	Dry UH
GB4133	AGSP-CYTEF	bluebunch wheatgrass-turpentine cymopterus	PCT	Hot dry UH	Dry UH

Table 9—Potential vegetation types (PVT) of the Blue Mountains section, organized by ecoclass code[a] (continued)

Ecoclass	PVT code (PLANTS code)	PVT common name	Status	PAG	PVG
GB4411	POBU-MAGL2	bulbous bluegrass-cluster tarweed	PCT	Hot dry UH	Dry UH
GB4911	AGSP-POSA12-DAUN	bluebunch wheatgrass-Sandberg's bluegrass-onespike oatgrass	PA	Hot dry UH	Dry UH
GB4915	BERE/AGSP-APAN2	creeping Oregongrape/bluebunch wheatgrass-spreading dogbane	PCT	Warm dry US	Dry US
GB5011	MEBU-STOC2	oniongrass-western needlegrass	PCT	Warm dry UH	Dry UH
GB5121	SYAL/FEID-AGSP-LUSE4	common snowberry/Idaho fescue-bluebunch wheatgrass-silky lupine	PCT	Warm moist US	Moist US
GB59	FEID-AGSP	Idaho fescue-bluebunch wheatgrass	PA	Warm moist UH	Moist UH
GB5911	FEID-KOCR (RIDGE)	Idaho fescue-prairie junegrass (ridge)	PA	Cool moist UH	Cold UH
GB5912	FEID-KOCR (MOUND)	Idaho fescue-prairie junegrass (mound)	PA	Cool moist UH	Cold UH
GB5913	FEID-KOCR (HIGH)	Idaho fescue-prairie junegrass (high elevation)	PA	Cool moist UH	Cold UH
GB5914	FEID-KOCR (LOW)	Idaho fescue-prairie junegrass (low elevation)	PA	Warm moist UH	Moist UH
GB5915	FEID-AGSP (RIDGE)	Idaho fescue-bluebunch wheatgrass (ridge)	PCT	Warm moist UH	Moist UH
GB5916	FEID-AGSP-LUPIN	Idaho fescue-bluebunch wheatgrass-lupine	PA	Warm moist UH	Moist UH
GB5917	FEID-AGSP-BASA3	Idaho fescue-bluebunch wheatgrass-arrowleaf balsamroot	PA	Warm moist UH	Moist UH
GB5918	FEID-AGSP-PHCO10	Idaho fescue-bluebunch wheatgrass-Snake River phlox	PA	Warm moist UH	Moist UH
GB5919	SYAL/FEID-KOCR	common snowberry/Idaho fescue-prairie junegrass	PCT	Warm moist US	Moist US
GB5920	FEID-DAIN-CAPE7	Idaho fescue-timber oatgrass-Liddon's sedge	PA	Warm very moist UH	Moist UH
GB5921	FEID-CAHO5	Idaho fescue-Hood's sedge	PA	Warm moist UH	Moist UH
GB5922	FEID-CAGE2	Idaho fescue-elk sedge	PCT	Warm moist UH	Moist UH
GB5923	FEID-GETR	Idaho fescue-red avens	PCT	Cool moist UH	Cold UH
GB5924	FEID-PESP2	Idaho fescue-Wallowa penstemon	PA	Cool moist UH	Cold UH
GB5925	FEID-AGSP-CYTEF	Idaho fescue-bluebunch wheatgrass-cymopterus	PA	Warm dry UH	Dry UH
GB5926	FEID-AGSP-FRALC2	Idaho fescue-bluebunch wheatgrass-Cusick's frasera	PA	Cool moist UH	Cold UH
GB5927	FEID-AGSP-PONEW	Idaho fescue-bluebunch wheatgrass-Wheeler's bluegrass	PC	Warm dry UH	Dry UH
GB5931	FEID-AGSP-PHLOX	Idaho fescue-bluebunch wheatgrass-phlox	PA	Warm moist UH	Moist UH
GB5932	FEID-DAUN	Idaho Fescue-onespike oatgrass	PCT	Warm dry UH	Dry UH
GB6011	FESC-FEID	rough fescue-Idaho fescue	PC	Cold dry UH	Cold UH
GB7111	ELCI2	basin wildrye	PCT	Hot very moist UH	Moist UH
GB9111	POSA12-DAUN	Sandberg's bluegrass-onespike oatgrass	PA	Hot dry UH	Dry UH
GB9112	POSA12-SELA	Sandberg's bluegrass-lanceleaf stonecrop	PC	Warm dry UH	Dry UH
GB9114	DAUN-LOLE2	onespike oatgrass-slenderfruit lomatium	PA	Hot moist UH	Moist UH
GM4111	CACA4	bluejoint reedgrass	PA	Cool moderate SM RH	Cold RH
GS10	STOC2	western needlegrass	PA	Cool moist UH	Cold UH
GS11	FEVI	green fescue	PCT	Cold moist UH	Cold UH
GS1111	FEVI-CAHO5	green fescue-Hood's sedge	PCT	Cold moist UH	Cold UH
GS1112	FEVI-LULA3	green fescue-spurred lupine	PA	Cold moist UH	Cold UH
GS1113	FEVI-JUPA	green fescue-Parry's rush	PA	Cold dry UH	Cold UH
GS1114	FEVI-CARO5	green fescue-Ross' sedge	PCT	Cold moist UH	Cold UH
GS1115	FEVI-PENST	green fescue-penstemon	PCT	Cold moist UH	Cold UH
GS1116	FEVI-STOC2	green fescue-western needlegrass	PCT	Cold moist UH	Cold UH
GS1117	FEVI-LICA2	green fescue-Canby's lovage	PC	Cold moist UH	Cold UH
GS1118	FEVI-AGCA2	green fescue-bearded wheatgrass	PC	Cold moist UH	Cold UH
GS1119	FEVI-CASC12	green fescue-Holm's Rocky Mountain sedge	PCT	Cold moist UH	Cold UH
GS12	FEID (ALPINE)	Idaho fescue (alpine)	PC	Cold dry UH	Cold UH
GS3912	CAGE2-FEID	elk sedge-Idaho fescue	PC	Cold dry UH	Cold UH

Table 9—Potential vegetation types (PVT) of the Blue Mountains section, organized by ecoclass code[a] (continued)

Ecoclass	PVT code (PLANTS code)	PVT common name	Status	PAG	PVG
GS3913	CAGE2-JUPA	elk sedge-Parry's rush	PC	Cold dry UH	Cold UH
GS3914	CAGE2-CARU	elk sedge-pinegrass	PC	Cold dry UH	Cold UH
GS3915	CAGE2-POCU3	elk sedge-Cusick's bluegrass	PC	Cold dry UH	Cold UH
GS3916	CAGE2-PHAU3	elk sedge-desert phlox	PC	Cold dry UH	Cold UH
GS3917	CAGE2-STOC2	elk sedge-western needlegrass	PC	Cold dry UH	Cold UH
GS4011	CAREX-STOC2	alpine sedges-western needlegrass	PC	Cold dry UH	Cold UH
GS4012	CAHO5-BRCA5 (MEADOW)	Hood's sedge-mountain brome (meadow)	PC	Cool moist UH	Cold UH
GS4013	JUPA-AGGL	Parry's rush-pale agoseris	PC	Cold dry UH	Cold UH
GS50	STOC2-SIHY (ALPINE)	western needlegrass-squirreltail (alpine)	PCT	Warm dry UH	Dry UH
GS60	FELLFIELD	fellfield	PC	Cold dry UH	Cold UH
GS61	CAHO5-BRCA5	Hood's sedge-mountain brome	PC	Cool moist UH	Cold UH
GS62	CAHO5-CAGE2	Hood's sedge-elk sedge	PC	Cool moist UH	Cold UH
GS63	CAHO5-POGL9	Hood's sedge-sticky cinquefoil	PC	Cool dry UH	Cold UH
GS64	CAHO5	Hood's sedge	PCT	Cool moist UH	Cold UH
GS70	TURF	turf	PC	Cold dry UH	Cold UH
HAF211	ALRU2/PEFRP	red alder/sweet coltsfoot	PCT	Warm moderate SM RF	Warm RF
HAF226	ALRU2 (ALLUVIAL BAR)	red alder (alluvial bar)	PCT	Warm moderate SM RF	Warm RF
HAF227	ALRU2/ATFI	red alder/ladyfern	PCT	Warm high SM RF	Warm RF
HAS211	ALRU2/PHCA11	red alder/Pacific ninebark	PA	Warm moderate SM RF	Warm RF
[none]	ALRU2/SYAL	red alder/common snowberry	PCT	Warm moderate SM RF	Warm RF
HAS312	ALRU2/SYAL/CADE9	red alder/common snowberry/Dewey's sedge	PCT	Warm moderate SM RF	Warm RF
HAS511	ALRU2/COST4	red alder/red osier dogwood	PC	Warm moderate SM RF	Warm RF
HCS112	POTR15/SALA5	black cottonwood/Pacific willow	PA	Hot moderate SM RF	Warm RF
HCS113	POTR15/ALIN2-COST4	black cottonwood/mountain alder-red osier dogwood	PA	Warm moderate SM RF	Warm RF
HCS114	POTR15/ACGL	black cottonwood/Rocky Mountain maple	PCT	Warm moderate SM RF	Warm RF
HCS311	POTR15/SYAL	black cottonwood/common snowberry	PCT	Hot moderate SM RF	Warm RF
HCS312	POTR15/SYAL	black cottonwood/common snowberry	PCT	Hot moderate SM RF	Warm RF
HD01	ACGL	Rocky Mountain maple	PCT	Hot low SM RS	Low SM RS
HQG112	POTR5/CAGE2	quaking aspen/elk sedge	PC	Cool very moist UF	Moist UF
HQM122	POTR5/POPR	quaking aspen/Kentucky bluegrass	PCT	Hot low SM RF	Low SM RF
HQM123	POTR5/CACA4	quaking aspen/bluejoint reedgrass	PCT	Warm moderate SM RF	Warm RF
HQM211	POTR5/CALA30	quaking aspen/woolly sedge	PA	Warm moderate SM RF	Warm RF
HQM212	POTR5/CAAQ	quaking aspen/aquatic sedge	PCT	Warm high SM RF	Warm RF
HQM511	POTR5/MESIC FORB	quaking aspen/mesic forb	PCT	Warm moderate SM RF	Warm RF
HQS221	POTR5/SYAL	quaking aspen/common snowberry	PCT	Hot moderate SM RF	Warm RF
HQS222	POTR5/ALIN2-COST4	quaking aspen/mountain alder-red osier dogwood	PCT	Warm moderate SM RF	Warm RF
HQS223	POTR5/ALIN2-SYAL	quaking aspen/mountain alder-common snowberry	PCT	Warm moderate SM RF	Warm RF
MD2111	ALPR3	meadow foxtail	PCT	Warm low SM RH	Low SM RH
MD3111	POPR (DRY MEADOW)	Kentucky bluegrass (dry meadow)	PCT	Warm low SM RH	Low SM RH
MD3112	POPR (DEGEN BENCH)	Kentucky bluegrass (degenerated bench)	PCT	Cool moist UH	Cold UH
MD4111	AGDI	thin bentgrass	PCT	Warm low SM RH	Low SM RH
MM1912	DECE	tufted hairgrass	PA	Cool moderate SM RH	Cold RH
MM2911	CALA30	woolly sedge	PA	Warm moderate SM RH	Warm RH
MM2912	CANE2	Nebraska sedge	PCT	Warm moderate SM RH	Warm RH
MM2913	CAEU2	widefruit sedge	PA	Cold high SM RH	Cold RH

Table 9—Potential vegetation types (PVT) of the Blue Mountains section, organized by ecoclass code[a] (continued)

Ecoclass	PVT code (PLANTS code)	PVT common name	Status	PAG	PVG
MM2914	CAAQ	aquatic sedge	PA	Cool high SM RH	Cold RH
MM2915	CASI2	shortbeaked sedge	PCT	Warm high SM RH	Warm RH
MM2916	CALU7	woodrush sedge	PA	Cold high SM RH	Cold RH
MM2917	CAUT	bladder sedge	PA	Cool high SM RH	Cold RH
MM2918	CACU5	Cusick's sedge	PA	Warm high SM RH	Warm RH
MM2919	CALE8	lakeshore sedge	PA	Warm moderate SM RH	Warm RH
MM2920	CALA11	slender sedge	PA	Warm high SM RH	Warm RH
MM2921	CAAM10	bigleaf sedge	PA	Warm high SM RH	Warm RH
MM2922	CANU5	torrent sedge	PCT	Hot high SM RH	Warm RH
MM2924	SCMI2	smallfruit bulrush	PA	Warm high SM RH	Warm RH
MM2925	GLEL	tall mannagrass	PA	Warm high SM RH	Warm RH
MM2926	PUPA3	weak alkaligrass	PA	Warm high SM RH	Warm RH
MM2927	CALE9	Sierra hare sedge	PA	Cold high SM RH	Cold RH
MM2928	CALI7	mud sedge	PA	Cold high SM RH	Cold RH
MM2929	CAMI7	smallwing sedge	PCT	Warm moderate SM RH	Warm RH
MM2930	CASU6	brown sedge	PC	Warm moderate SM RH	Warm RH
MM2932	CASH	Sheldon's sedge	PCT	Hot moderate SM RH	Warm RH
MM2933	CAJO	Jones' sedge	PC	Warm moderate SM RH	Warm RH
MS2111	CANI2	black alpine sedge	PA	Cold moderate SM RH	Cold RH
MS2113	CASC10-SAAR13	northern singlespike sedge-brook saxifrage	PA	Cold high SM RH	Cold RH
MS3111	CASC12	Holm's Rocky Mountain Sedge	PA	Warm moderate SM RH	Warm RH
MS3112	CAMU7	star sedge	PCT	Warm moderate SM RH	Warm RH
MS3113	CACA11	silvery sedge	PCT	Warm moderate SM RH	Warm RH
MS4111	ELBE	delicate spikerush	PC	Cold high SM RH	Cold RH
MT10	NUPO2	Rocky Mountain pondlily	PA	Cool high SM RH	Cold RH
MT8121	TYLA	common cattail	PC	Hot high SM RH	Warm RH
MW1923	CAVE6	inflated sedge	PA	Cool high SM RH	Cold RH
MW1926	CAST5	sawbeak sedge	PCT	Warm high SM RH	Warm RH
MW2912	CAPR5	clustered field sedge	PCT	Cold high SM RH	Cold RH
MW2913	CALA13	smoothstemmed sedge	PA	Cold high SM RH	Cold RH
MW2927	CILA2	drooping woodreed	PC	Cold high SM RH	Cold RH
MW3912	JUBA	Baltic rush	PCT	Warm moderate SM RH	Warm RH
MW4911	ELPA6	fewflowered spikerush	PA	Cold high SM RH	Cold RH
MW4912	ELPA3	creeping spikerush	PA	Hot high SM RH	Warm RH
NTS111	PHLE4 (TALUS)	syringa-bordered talus strips	PCT	Hot very moist US	Moist US
SD01	ARLU	white sagebrush	PCT	Warm low SM RH	Low SM RH
SD1911	ARAR8/FEID-AGSP	low sagebrush/Idaho fescue-bluebunch wheatgrass	PA	Warm moist US	Moist US
SD1924	ARAR8/AGSP	low sagebrush/bluebunch wheatgrass	PA	Warm dry US	Dry US
SD2401	ARTR4/POSA12-DAUN	threetip sagebrush/Sandberg's bluegrass-onespike oatgrass	PCT	Warm dry US	Dry US
SD2911	ARTRV/FEID-AGSP	mountain big sagebrush/Idaho fescue-bluebunch wheatgrass	PA	Warm moist US	Moist US
SD2915	ARTRV/CAGE2 (MONTANE)	mountain big sagebrush/elk sedge (montane)	PCT	Warm moist US	Moist US
SD2916	ARTRV-PUTR2/FEID	mountain big sagebrush-bitterbrush/Idaho fescue	PCT	Hot moist US	Moist US
SD2917	ARTRV-SYOR2/BRCA5	mountain big sagebrush-mountain snowberry/mountain brome	PCT	Warm moist US	Moist US
SD2918	ARTRV/AGSP-POSA12	mountain big sagebrush/bluebunch wheatgrass-Sandberg's bluegrass	PA	Warm dry US	Dry US

Table 9—Potential vegetation types (PVT) of the Blue Mountains section, organized by ecoclass code[a] (continuexd)

Ecoclass	PVT code (PLANTS code)	PVT common name	Status	PAG	PVG
SD2919	ARTRV-SYOR2	mountain big sagebrush-mountain snowberry	PCT	Warm moist US	Moist US
SD2920	ARTRV/STOC2	mountain big sagebrush/western needlegrass	PC	Cool dry US	Cold US
SD2929	ARTRV/FEID-KOCR	mountain big sagebrush/Idaho fescue-prairie junegrass	PA	Warm moist US	Moist US
SD30	PERA4-SYOR2	squaw apple-mountain snowberry	PCT	Hot moist US	Moist US
SD3010	ARTRV-PERA4	mountain big sagebrush-squaw apple	PCT	Warm moist US	Moist US
SD3011	ARTRV/ELCI2	mountain big sagebrush/basin wildrye	PCT	Warm moist US	Moist US
SD3111	PUTR2/FEID-AGSP	bitterbrush/Idaho fescue-bluebunch wheatgrass	PA	Warm moist US	Moist US
SD3112	PUTR2/AGSP	bitterbrush/bluebunch wheatgrass	PA	Hot moist US	Moist US
SD3124	PUTR2-ARTRV/FEID-AGSP	bitterbrush-mountain big sagebrush/Idaho fescue-bluebunch wheatgrass	PA	Warm moist US	Moist US
SD3125	PUTR2-ARTRV/FEID	bitterbrush-mountain big sagebrush/Idaho fescue	PCT	Warm moist US	Moist US
SD3126	PUTR2/ERDO	bitterbrush/Douglas' buckwheat	PCT	Warm dry US	Dry US
SD40	CELE3/CAGE2	mountain mahogany/elk sedge	PC	Warm moist US	Moist US
SD4111	CELE3/FEID-AGSP	mountain mahogany/Idaho fescue-bluebunch wheatgrass	PA	Warm moist US	Moist US
SD4112	CELE3/AGSP	mountain mahogany/bluebunch wheatgrass	PCT	Warm dry US	Dry US
SD4113	CELE3/CAGE2	mountain mahogany/elk sedge	PC	Warm dry US	Dry US
SD4114	CELE3/PONEW	mountain mahogany/Wheeler's bluegrass	PCT	Warm dry US	Dry US
SD4115	CELE3-PUTR2/AGSP	mountain mahogany-bitterbrush/bluebunch wheatgrass	PCT	Warm moist US	Moist US
SD49	CELE3	mountain mahogany	PCT	Warm dry US	Dry US
SD5611	CERE2/AGSP	netleaf hackberry/bluebunch wheatgrass	PA	Hot moist US	Moist US
SD5612	CERE2/BROMU	netleaf hackberry/brome	PCT	Hot low SM RS	Low SM RS
SD6121	RHGL/AGSP	smooth sumac/bluebunch wheatgrass	PA	Hot dry US	Dry US
SD65	GLSPA/AGSP	spiny greasebush/bluebunch wheatgrass	PA	Hot dry US	Dry US
SD9111	ARRI2/POSA12 (SCAB)	stiff sagebrush/Sandberg's bluegrass (scabland)	PA	Warm dry US	Dry US
SD9141	ARRI2/PEGA	stiff sagebrush/Gairdner's penstemon	PCT	Warm dry US	Dry US
SD9221	ARAR8/POSA12	low sagebrush/Sandberg's bluegrass	PA	Warm dry US	Dry US
SD9322	ERIOG-PHOR2	buckwheat/Oregon bladderpod	PA	Hot dry UH	Dry UH
SM1111	PHMA5-SYAL	mallow ninebark-common snowberry	PCT	Warm moist US	Moist US
SM19	PHMA5-SYAL	mallow ninebark-common snowberry	PCT	Warm moist US	Moist US
SM1901	PHCA11	Pacific ninebark	PC	Warm low SM RS	Low SM RS
SM20	ALSI3	alder snow slides	PCT	Cold very moist US	Cold US
SM3001	PHLE4/MESIC FORB	Lewis' mockorange/mesic forb	PCT	Hot low SM RS	Low SM RS
SM31	SYAL	common snowberry	PCT	Warm moist US	Moist US
SM3110	SYAL (FLOODPLAIN)	common snowberry (floodplain)	PCT	Hot moderate SM RS	Warm RS
SM3111	SYAL-ROSA5	common snowberry-rose	PCT	Warm moist US	Moist US
SM32	SYOR2	mountain snowberry	PCT	Warm moist US	Moist US
SM33	CEVE	snowbrush ceanothus	PCT	Warm moist US	Moist US
SM34	PREM	bitter cherry	PC	Warm moist US	Moist US
SM41	BEOC2/PHAR3	water birch/reed canarygrass	PC	Warm moderate SM RS	Warm RS
SM5001	RUBA	Barton's raspberry	PC	Hot low SM RS	Low SM RS
SM5002	RUDI2	Himalayan blackberry	PC	Hot moderate SM RS	Warm RS
SM5912	RUPA	thimbleberry	PCT	Hot moderate SM RS	Warm RS
SS1912	PHEM (MOUNDS)	pink mountainheath (mounds)	PA	Cold moderate SM RS	Cold RS
SS4911	ARTRV/CAGE2	mountain big sagebrush/elk sedge	PA	Cold moist US	Cold US
SS4914	ARTRV/BRCA5	mountain big sagebrush/mountain brome	PCT	Warm moist US	Moist US

85

Table 9—Potential vegetation types (PVT) of the Blue Mountains section, organized by ecoclass code[a] (continued)

Ecoclass	PVT code (PLANTS code)	PVT common name	Status	PAG	PVG
SS4915	ARTRV/FEVI	mountain big sagebrush/green fescue	PCT	Cold moist US	Cold US
SS4916	ARTRV/CAHO5	mountain big sagebrush/Hood's sedge	PCT	Cold moist US	Cold US
SS4917	ARTRV/LINU4	mountain big sagebrush/linanthus	PCT	Cool dry US	Cold US
SS4918	ARTRV/ERFL4-PHLOX	mountain big sagebrush/golden buckwheat-phlox	PC	Cool dry US	Cold US
SS4919	POFR4/FEID	shrubby cinquefoil/Idaho fescue	PCT	Warm moist US	Moist US
SS60	POFR4	shrubby cinquefoil	PC	Cool moist US	Cold US
SS6001	POFR4-BEGL	shrubby cinquefoil-bog birch	PCT	Cold moderate SM RS	Cold RS
SW0101	LEGL/CASC12	Labrador tea/Holm's Rocky Mountain sedge	PC	Cold moderate SM RS	Cold RS
SW0102	LOIN5/ATFI	twinberry honeysuckle/ladyfern	PC	Warm moderate SM RS	Warm RS
SW1111	SALIX/POPR	willow/Kentucky bluegrass	PCT	Warm low SM RS	Low SM RS
SW1112	SALIX/CALA30	willow/woolly sedge	PA	Warm moderate SM RS	Warm RS
SW1114	SALIX/CAAQ	willow/aquatic sedge	PA	Cool high SM RS	Cold RS
SW1117	SAEX	coyote willow	PA	Warm moderate SM RS	Warm RS
SW1121	SACO2/CASC12	undergreen willow/Holm's Rocky Mountain sedge	PA	Cold high SM RS	Cold RS
SW1123	SALIX/CAUT	willow/bladder sedge	PA	Warm high SM RS	Warm RS
SW1124	SALIX/CACA4	willow/bluejoint reedgrass	PA	Cool moderate SM RS	Cold RS
SW1125	SALIX/MESIC FORB	willow/mesic forb	PCT	Warm moderate SM RS	Warm RS
SW1126	SARI2	rigid willow	PCT	Hot moderate SM RS	Warm RS
SW1127	SACO2/CAUT	undergreen willow/bladder sedge	PCT	Cold high SM RS	Cold RS
SW1128	SACO2/CAPR5	undergreen willow/clustered field sedge	PC	Cold high SM RS	Cold RS
SW1129	SAEA-SATW/CAAQ	Eastwood willow-Tweedy willow/aquatic sedge	PC	Warm high SM RS	Warm RS
SW1130	SASC/ELGL	Scouler's willow/blue wildrye	PC	Warm low SM RS	Low SM RS
SW1133	SAAR27	arctic willow	PA	Cold high SM RS	Cold RS
SW1134	SAFA/ALVA	Farr's willow/Pacific onion	PC	Cold high SM RS	Cold RS
SW1135	SALE/MESIC FORB	Lemmon's willow/mesic forb	PCT	Warm moderate SM RS	Warm RF
SW1136	SASI2/EQAR	Sitka willow/common horsetail	PC	Warm high SM RS	Warm RS
SW1137	SADR/SETR	Drummond's willow/arrowleaf groundsel	PC	Cold high SM RS	Cold RS
SW1138	SABO2/CASC12	Booth's willow/Holm's Rocky Mountain sedge	PA	Cold high SM RS	Cold RS
SW1139	SABO2/CAVE6	Booth's willow/inflated sedge	PC	Cold high SM RS	Cold RS
SW2101	ALRH2/RUBUS	white alder/blackberry	PCT	Hot moderate SM RF	Warm RF
SW2102	ALRH2/MESIC SHRUB	white alder/mesic shrub	PCT	Hot moderate SM RF	Warm RF
SW2111	ALSI3/ATFI	Sitka alder/ladyfern	PA	Warm high SM RS	Warm RS
SW2112	ALSI3/CILA2	Sitka alder/drooping woodreed	PA	Warm high SM RS	Warm RS
SW2113	ALSI3/MESIC FORB	Sitka alder/mesic forb	PCT	Warm moderate SM RS	Warm RS
SW2114	ALIN2/CAAM10	mountain alder/bigleaf sedge	PA	Warm high SM RS	Warm RS
SW2115	ALIN2/CAUT	mountain alder/bladder sedge	PA	Warm high SM RS	Warm RS
SW2116	ALIN2/ATFI	mountain alder/ladyfern	PA	Warm high SM RS	Warm RS
SW2117	ALIN2/EQAR	mountain alder/common horsetail	PA	Warm moderate SM RS	Warm RS
SW2118	ALIN2/CADE9	mountain alder/Dewey's sedge	PCT	Warm moderate SM RS	Warm RS
SW2120	ALIN2/POPR	mountain alder/Kentucky bluegrass	PCT	Warm low SM RS	Low SM RS
SW2121	ALIN2/CACA4	mountain alder/bluejoint reedgrass	PA	Warm moderate SM RS	Warm RS
SW2122	ALIN2/SCMI2	mountain alder/smallfruit bulrush	PCT	Warm high SM RS	Warm RS
SW2123	ALIN2/CALA30	mountain alder/woolly sedge	PA	Warm moderate SM RS	Warm RS
SW2124	ALIN2/HELA4	mountain alder/common cowparsnip	PCT	Warm moderate SM RS	Warm RS

Table 9—Potential vegetation types (PVT) of the Blue Mountains section, organized by ecoclass code[a] (continued)

Ecoclass	PVT code (PLANTS code)	PVT common name	Status	PAG	PVG
SW2125	ALIN2/GYDR	mountain alder/oakfern	PCT	Warm moderate SM RS	Warm RS
SW2126	ALIN2/CAAQ	mountain alder/aquatic sedge	PC	Warm high SM RS	Warm RS
SW2127	ALIN2/CALEL	mountain alder/densely tufted sedge	PC	Warm moderate SM RS	Warm RS
SW2128	ALIN2/CALU7	mountain alder/woodrush sedge	PC	Warm low SM RS	Low SM RS
SW2211	ALIN2-SYAL	mountain alder-common snowberry	PA	Warm low SM RS	Low SM RS
SW2215	ALIN2/GLEL	mountain alder/tall mannagrass	PA	Warm high SM RS	Warm RS
SW2216	ALIN2-COST4/MESIC FORB	mountain alder-red osier dogwood/mesic forb	PA	Warm moderate SM RS	Warm RS
SW2217	ALIN2-RIBES/MESIC FORB	mountain alder-currants/mesic forb	PA	Warm moderate SM RS	Warm RS
SW3111	CRDO2/MESIC FORB	black hawthorn/mesic forb	PCT	Hot low SM RS	Low SM RS
SW3112	BEOC2/MESIC FORB	water birch/mesic forb	PCT	Warm moderate SM RS	Warm RS
SW3113	BEOC2/WET SEDGE	water birch/wet sedge	PCT	Warm high SM RS	Warm RS
SW3114	AMAL2	western serviceberry	PCT	Hot low SM RS	Low SM RS
SW3124	HELA4-ELGL	common cowparsnip/blue wildrye	PC	Warm moderate SM RH	Warm RH
SW4133	COST4/ATFI	red osier dogwood/ladyfern	PA	Warm high SM RS	Warm RS
SW5111	RIBES/CILA2	currants/drooping woodreed	PCT	Warm high SM RS	Warm RS
SW5112	COST4	red osier dogwood	PA	Warm moderate SM RS	Warm RS
SW5113	POFR4/DECE	shrubby cinquefoil/tufted hairgrass	PA	Warm moderate SM RS	Warm RS
SW5114	POFR4/POPR	shrubby cinquefoil/Kentucky bluegrass	PCT	Warm low SM RS	Low SM RS
SW5115	RIBES/MESIC FORB	currants/mesic forb	PCT	Warm moderate SM RS	Warm RS
SW5116	RIBES/GLEL	currants/tall mannagrass	PCT	Warm high SM RS	Warm RS
SW5117	RHAL/MESIC FORB	alderleaf buckthorn/mesic forb	PCT	Warm moderate SM RS	Warm RS
SW5118	COST4/SAAR13	red osier dogwood/brook saxifrage	PCT	Warm high SM RS	Warm RS
SW6111	ARCA13/DECE	silver sagebrush/tufted hairgrass	PA	Hot moderate SM RS	Warm RS
SW6112	ARCA13/POPR	silver sagebrush/Kentucky bluegrass	PCT	Hot low SM RS	Low SM RS
SW6113	ARTRV/POCU3	mountain big sagebrush/Cusick's bluegrass	PA	Hot low SM RS	Low SM RS
SW6114	ARCA13/POCU3	silver sagebrush/Cusick's bluegrass	PCT	Hot low SM RS	Low SM RS
SW901	KAMI/CANI2	alpine laurel/black alpine sedge	PA	Cold high SM RS	Cold RS
WL0108	SPAN2	narrowleaf bur-reed	PA	Cold high SM RH	Cold RH

[a] This tabular summary is organized alphabetically by ecoclass code (USDA Forest Service 2002). Column descriptions are the same as for appendix table 8.

PAG = plant association group, PVG = potential vegetation group.